Bushcraft
Whittling

Rick Wiebe

LINDEN PUBLISHING

Bushcraft Whittling
© copyright Rick Wiebe 2021

All rights reserved. No part of this book may be reproduced or transmitted in any form or by any means, electronic or mechanical, including photocopying, recording, or by an information storage and retrieval system, without written permission from the publisher.

Interior layout by Carla Green, Clarity Designworks

ISBN: 978-161035-992-4

1 3 5 7 9 8 6 4 2

Woodworking is inherently dangerous. Your safety is your responsibility. Neither Linden Publishing nor the author assume any responsibility for any injuries or accidents.

Linden Publishing titles may be purchased in quantity at special discounts for educational, business, or promotional use. To inquire about discount pricing, please refer to the contact information below. For permission to use any portion of this book for academic purposes, please contact the Copyright Clearance Center at www.copyright.com

Printed in the United States of America

Library of Congress Cataloging-in-Publication data on file

Linden Publishing, Inc.
2006 S. Mary
Fresno, CA 93721
www.lindenpub.com

Contents

Introduction v

Chapter 1 ~ Tools of the Craft...1

Chapter 2 ~ Sharpening..11

Chapter 3 ~ Ways of Cutting..27

Chapter 4 ~ Simple Disposable Items 49

Chapter 5 ~ Treen 61

Chapter 6 ~ Walking Sticks, Canes, and Crutches 83

Chapter 7 ~ Walking Sticks with Personality......................95

Chapter 8 ~ Eyes 141

Chapter 9 ~ Whittling Bushcraft Tools............................. 151

Chapter 10 ~ Toys 163

About the Author 191

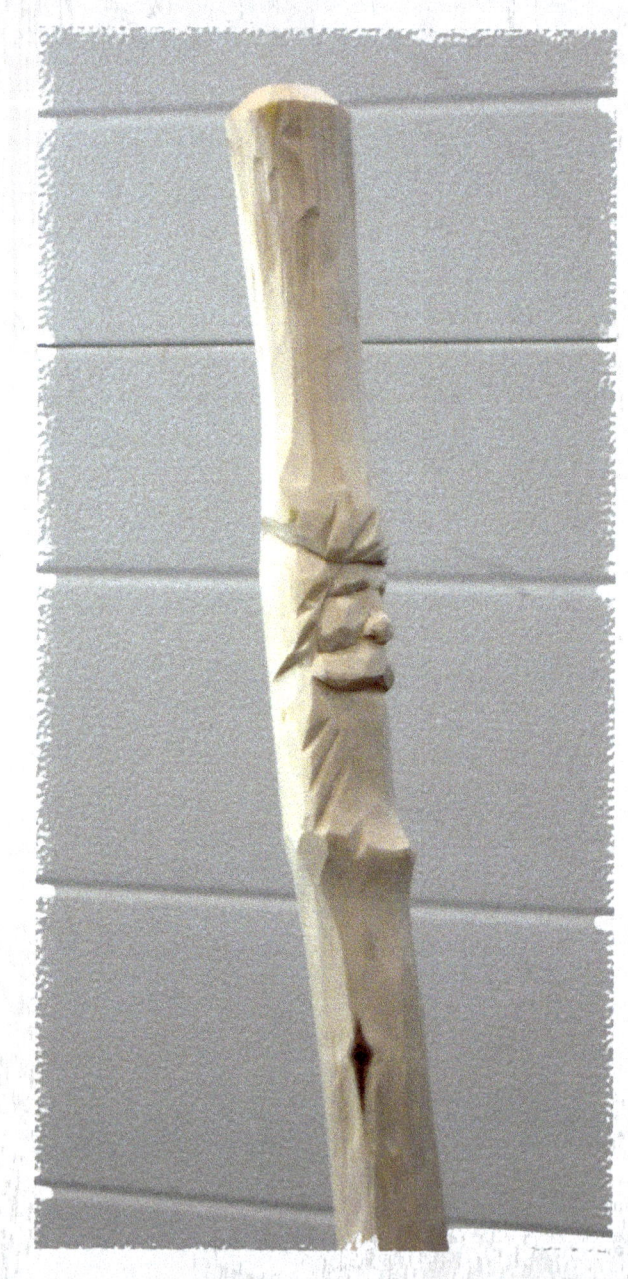

Introduction

Sixty-five years ago, I was a bushcraft whittler. I did not know it at the time, because "bushcraft" wasn't even a word. I do not remember if I even thought of myself as a whittler. I just did it.

"I'm going to the bush with Sandy" was what I told Mom as I headed out the door. Sandy was my best friend who lived a block away. Half a block away was a big patch of forest—the bush. We had great times building "forts," pretending we were Robin Hood or Davy Crockett, getting dirty, and just having as much fun as a couple of boys could.

Whittlin' with knife, axe, and saw was always a part of these adventures, and we often brought materials gathered in the bush home to continue our projects.

We had no instruction. We just got an idea and tried it, and as we did, our skills grew and our projects even, sometimes, started to look like what we had envisioned. It was great fun.

I never outgrew it.

It actually has become kind of an obsession. I always have at least one knife with me. Trees tremble when I approach—especially aspens. I indulge in this three-dimensional doodling whenever I can. It's fun, and I have found that lots of other people, with a little instruction and encouragement, enjoy it too.

It has never been easier to get all kinds of information, instruction, and ideas on pretty much anything that can be imagined and several things that seem unimaginable! Bushcraft and whittlin' are amazingly well represented on YouTube. A lot of the information there is very good.

While the information and inspiration is easy to obtain, it might be a lot harder now for today's budding whittler to actually *do it*.

This book was written in the hope that readers will get inspired to go beyond the ideas, and gear, and *do it*!

I really hope that these pages will give you some basic information that will speed up the learning process, but more than anything I would like to give you a little nudge, even a push.

Just *do it*!

CHAPTER 1

~~~

Tools of the Craft

Only a few tools are necessary to do bushcraft whittlin', but having the right ones in the right condition will make the work easier and a *lot* more fun.

The basic bushcraft tools—knife, axe, and saw—are really all that are needed to get started. If you have been doing some bushcrafting already, you will be able to use what you have, but here are a few things that might be worth considering.

FIRST THINGS FIRST

You can't whittle without a sharp knife, so let's start there. Most bushcrafters have and use a simple sheath knife, and it is hard to beat a Mora knife. They come in several models and sizes, but any of them, except for the really big ones, will serve for the projects in this book.

On the following pages, I'll show you some of my favorites, why I like them, and what you might in your personal toolkit.

A quick word about sheaths: Have nothing to do with carrying a knife in a sheath that can be bent with the fingers, as shown in this photo. Very unsafe.

Moras are sometimes criticized for their sheaths, mostly because they are not leather (horrors!), but they are very functional and safe. Many leather ones that come with even expensive knives are not safe. Actually, the sheath is one of the great things about a Mora. It has no straps and snaps, and that facilitates accessing and replacing the knife with one hand. Ease of doing these routine things helps prevent loss, since most lost knives are walked away from, not dropped.

Some people prefer a folding knife. A large folder with one or two blades can do pretty much everything that a non-folder will do. Actually, a jumbo stock knife with three blades, especially one modified like the one in this photo, might be able to do every bushcraft task that is required. I would not feel at all handicapped if that was the only knife I had for bushcraft and bushcraft whittlin'.

A smaller knife is very desirable for any kind of detailed whittlin'. The rule of thumb is to use the smallest blade that will do the job, because smaller blades are easier to control, and control is really what it's all about. With that in mind, the bushcraft whittler will find it very helpful to have, in addition to the regular all-purpose bushcraft knife, a smaller pocketknife with two or three blades, like the ones below. If the blades have been modified a bit to make them even more useful for whittlin', so much the better. Compare the knives in these photos.

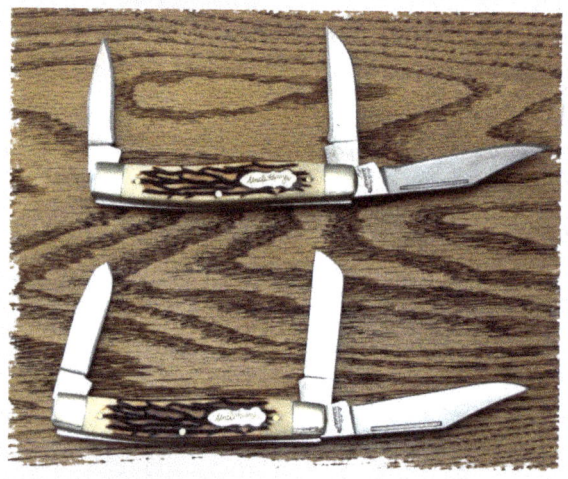

It is easy to see that the top one has been modified. These alterations are not at all difficult to accomplish. A good file and a sharpening stone are all that a handy person (and bushcrafters are the embodiment of "handy people") will need to do the job.

This Swiss Army knife, with two blades that have been slightly modified, and an awl, might just be the perfect pocketknife for the bushcraft whittler.

~ *Tools of the Craft* ~

The single-bladed Opinel #8 below makes a good bushcrafting knife and the modified one makes a good secondary one. Very inexpensive but very good!

A saw is very useful for bushcrafting, to the point of being almost essential. Lots of different bow and folding saws will do the job, but the pictured ones are the handiest. The small one fits in the hip pocket (closed!) and does a lot! The big one will handle the big stuff. A chain saw, of course, will do a lot more, and faster, but isn't nearly as portable. It is possible to make a buck saw too, and that will be covered in the chapter devoted to making bushcrafting tools.

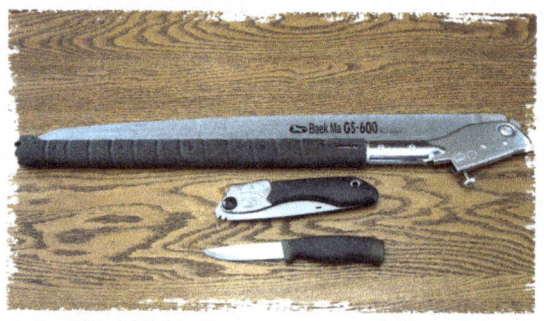

Some bushcrafters say they do not need or want an axe. Heresy! There are some of us who would sooner be without a knife than a hatchet or an axe. Some very fine work can be done with an axe, and it can do heavy work that would be nearly impossible with a knife, unless that knife is big and heavy enough to pretty much be an axe in a different format.

~ Tools of the Craft ~

The colder and snowier the environment, the more the axe, and the bigger the axe, that is needed. Nothing gets firewood for large and sustained fires like an axe, coupled with a saw, and those two tools make it possible to get the kind of materials needed for whittlin' too.

Here are a couple of axes that serve the bushcrafter and whittler well.

The smaller one rides in the day pack that goes everywhere and is a good whittlin' tool in itself. The larger one has been in my possession for about 60 years (it's on its third handle) and has done an amazing amount of work. It is what is often called a "boy's axe." Larger axes have their uses too. Some people like double-bit axes, but they are very specialized tools for expert users. Most bushcrafters will have no need for them.

MEET YOUR MULTITOOL

A multi-tool like the Leatherman pictured below is very useful. Several other brands work well too. This one goes everywhere but to church!

The knife blades on it are somewhat awkward, not at all useful as the primary bushcrafting knife, and certainly not at all useful as the detailing pocketknife. But the pliers, wire cutters, and other tools are quite handy.

The Leatherman comes in a portable and compact package. Many multi-tools have a diamond file, which is a good sharpening "stone" for knives and axes. They usually have a surprisingly effective saw too, the back of which makes a great scraper for wood and for making sparks from a ferrocerium rod ("fire-steel") for starting campfires. Do not get a cheapie! Cheap multi-tools are worse than none.

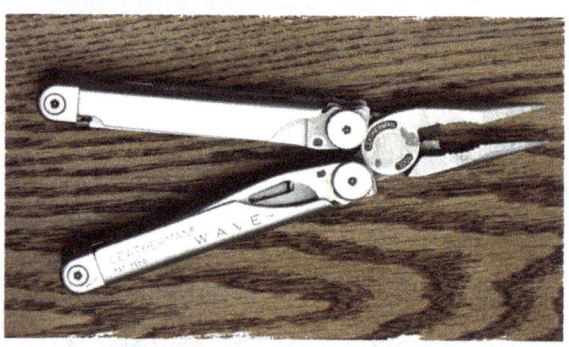

If spoons, ladles, and cups are planned projects, then a gouge or two and/or a bent knife, like the set pictured on the opposite page, are important.

~ Tools of the Craft ~

Lots of spoons and cups have been made without these tools, but the process would have been a lot easier and the products a *lot* better with them. Please note that the bent knives come in right- and left-handed versions. Most people need only one.

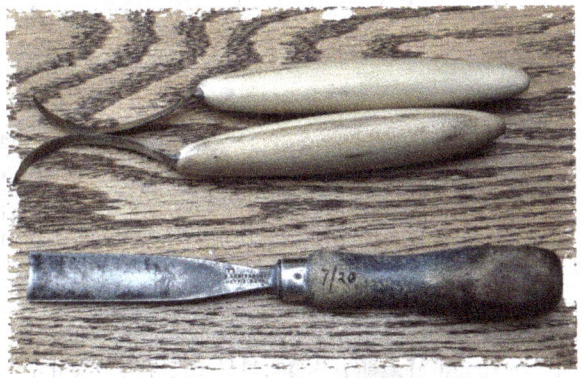

Here are a couple of example "kits" that would serve the bushcraft whittler well.

We still need an axe in the set pictured above, of course. There's a small folding saw, but I would also add that big folding saw shown previously. I wish I could've had that large folding saw about 40 years earlier!

CHAPTER 2

~~~

Sharpening

This is important stuff coming up. Do not skip it! Sharp tools will make whittlin' and all other bushcrafting fun. Dull or even just-not-so-sharp tools can make it into an ordeal.

"Wow! That knife is really sharp!" An expert whittler hears that a lot. If he or she doesn't, then maybe the expertise is lacking. Dull knives are utterly useless! Here is how to prevent and/or correct that deplorable situation.

There is no such thing as a knife that will stay sharp forever. Most knives will not be very sharp when they are purchased, though there are exceptions.

For example, Moras come usably sharp and are among the easiest to keep that way, so let's start there.

Well actually, it will be necessary to comment on something else first: sharpening stones. "Stones" really, because, while it is possible to get stones that are not man-made, there are better and less expensive options available today.

STARTER STONES

The simplest way to get a sharpening stone is just to go and buy one. Sadly, this will be very confusing for the beginner, since many of the sharpening devices available really don't work very well, and it is hard for a beginner to know which of them will work.

If the seller has a knife on him (if he doesn't have one on him, he is not a knife person—so move along) that he can shave with, that is a good sign! Such a person probably knows about good stones and will be able to steer you right. Unfortunately, many vendors do not.

Attending a carving club meeting or two would probably be useful, though, weirdly, not everyone there will know how to sharpen well. Somebody will, though and will be a good source of advice.

THE DIY OPTION

A pretty good sharpening stone can be made with some flat pieces of plywood about 2" wide by 8" long and some wet or dry sandpaper which you should be able to find at most hardware stores.

Start by getting a couple of sheets of 120 grit, a couple of 220 grit, and three or four sheets of 440 grit. It wouldn't be a bad idea to get some 600 grit too. Get some two-sided carpet tape while you are at it, which comes in 2" widths. Stick some 2"-wide strips of the sandpaper down to the boards to make quite functional sharpening boards.

~ Sharpening ~

The sandpaper works well but wears out pretty quickly, and because of that it can wind up costing more than a stone. But sandpaper will be available at a lot of places where it will be impossible to find a good stone.

Here are some things that are useful for sharpening.

A sandpaper stone is at the bottom of the photo.

Resist the temptation to get a sharpening stone from the hardware store that costs less than $25. If that store has a Norton India stone, coarse black silicon carbide on one side and fine orangish aluminum oxide on the other side, grab it! It needs to be at least 6" long; 8" is better and 10" is really good but not necessary. It will not be inexpensive, but it will be worth it and functional for many years.

An aluminum oxide stone is the orange-brownish item second from the bottom in the photo.

The next item is a ceramic rod. More on that later.
Then a diamond stone.

Most cities have a discount tool outlet. You know, the ones that have seaports and freight in their name. In Canada, they mention royalty and cars. Odd. Anyway, these places have some quite inexpensive diamond sharpening stones that come in kits with 3 or 4 grits (see picture below). These are surprisingly good, and while they are not as good as more expensive diamond stones, they will do the job. Get ones that are 6" or 8" long and 1½" to 2" wide.

While at the discount store, try to get a small stick or sometimes a paper tube of green or white buffing compound. Do not get red. Red is almost useless for sharpening knives.

Read and understand these instructions carefully before beginning.

~ Sharpening ~

Back to the Mora. Moras are ground with what is usually called a Scandi edge. Short for Scandinavian. This is the wide bevel that tapers down to the cutting edge, as shown here. That bevel creates a built-in sharpening guide.

Begin by laying the bevel flat on the stone.

If the Mora is new, it won't need the coarser grits and probably could just be used the way it comes from the store, but sooner or later you will need to sharpen it. If the knife is really dull, it will be helpful to start with the coarser grits and work through to the finer ones.

Next, move the blade back and forth on the stone, keeping the bevel flat on the surface of the stone. Use a fair bit of pressure. If you have the diamond stone or the sandpaper, you can put some water on the surface of the stone and keep it wet while going through this process. They can be used dry too. If you have the Norton, it will come oil-filled, and you will need to keep the stone wet with oil. Baby oil works great and is inexpensive.

Do not turn the knife over and sharpen the other side until a burr can be felt all along the edge on the side that is not contacting the stone. **do not** slide your finger down the edge checking for the burr, lest you bleed. To check for the burr, touch the edge on the side that was *not* in contact with the stone, and push away from the edge. Pushing into the edge will extract blood.

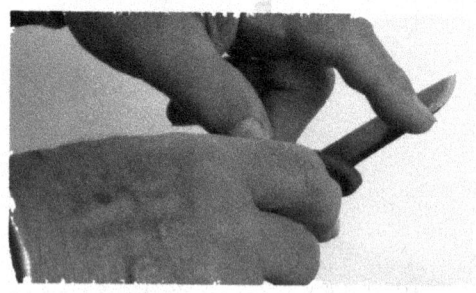

~ Sharpening ~

Do not quit on the one side until that burr is produced. When it has been produced, turn the knife over and repeat on the other side of the blade until the burr is again raised all along the edge on the other side. This burr is often referred to as "the wire edge."

ANGLE CONTROL

If the knife that is being sharpened does not have a Scandi edge like a Mora, then hold the blade at about a 10- to 15-degree angle and try to maintain that as the process goes on. A nickel or a quarter laid on the stone can be a useful spacer to help get the correct angle, as shown below.

If a little 10-degree wedge can be made, it will be really useful in holding that correct angle. The photo on the next page shows an example of what I'm talking about.

I make these sharpening wedges by the hundreds and give them to everyone who buys a stone and also to lots of people who don't buy anything.

In this whole process, the blade will get scratched. Do not be alarmed. We want to cut with this, not look at it. Do not be afraid that the knife will be ruined. It is very difficult to ruin a knife with hand stones. However, it is very easy to wreck it on a powered grindstone. Do not even contemplate it! If a person did wreck a knife (which is very unlikely) but learned to sharpen in the process, it would be worth it.

After raising the burr on the second side, go to a finer grit and repeat the whole process. When the process has been done on the finest stone, put the burr down at the same angle and give it a few light rubs. Then turn it over and do a few light rubs on the other side. Repeat until no burr is felt.

CRAFTING A STROP

Now it is time to strop, which will remove a microscopic wire edge that is very hard to feel but is present and will fold over or rip off when the knife is in use, leaving the knife duller than it should be.

Strops have been traditionally made with leather, but it has been discovered that denim, as from an old pair of blue jeans, works just as well and in some cases better. Besides, everybody can come up with some denim, but a good piece of leather could be difficult to find.

To create your strop, start with a 2"-wide piece of plywood about 8" or 10" long. Now, remember that two-sided carpet tape you purchased (or more likely dug out of a drawer or toolkit) to make your DIY sharpening stone, as described on page 12? Take a piece of tape as long as your board and stick it to the wood. Cut a piece of denim 2½" wide, peel off the backing on the exposed side of the tape and stick the denim down, leaving ¼" overhang on the sides and ends. The overhang prevents excessive fraying. Now, using the green or white buffing compound (see page 14) like a crayon, coat the strop. This will be enough compound to sharpen 100–200 blades. Really!

NOW YOU'RE STROPPING

Put the blade on the strop at the same angle at which it was sharpened. Flat on the bevel for the Mora. Use quite a lot of pressure, and *pull* the knife along the strop. Do not cut into the strop. Drag the edge. There is no need to try to strop the entire edge on every stroke, just work across with subsequent strokes so that the entire edge gets done.

Do not give the knife a little flip at the end of the stroke, or go one way and then back the other way. If you do, you will anticipate that flip and drag the edge at too high an angle and make the knife dull, not sharp.

~ Sharpening ~

Never touch the strop at an angle like this:

Just give one side of the blade about 50 to 75 firm strokes with no flip—and do not run off the end of the strop either. Maintain the sharpening angle for the entire stroke. Then turn the knife over and do the other side.

The knife should now be shaving-sharp.

SHARPENING WITH CERAMIC

As a finishing touch, you'll want to give the edge a bit of "tooth," which will help your just-sharpened edge to cut for a while longer.

The best way to do this is with a couple of strokes at the same angle or maybe a 1- or 2-degree steeper angle on a ceramic stick, or on the bottom of a porcelain mug, as shown below.

When the edge is lost a bit in use, the ceramic rod or mug can be used again to make the edge come back. After a few treatments like this, some more stropping and ceramic will be needed, and when that edge lasts only a few minutes, back to the stone again.

This sharpening thing will take a while for you to "get it," but with practice it will happen a lot more quickly.

Now go sharpen everything in sight. Help stamp out dullness!

~ Sharpening ~

Make sure the back (or spine) of the Mora or other sheath knife has nice sharp corners. These will be useful in fire lighting and as a scraper for making wood nice and smooth.

Use a flat file to square up the back of the knife blade. This is easier to do if you have a vise, but if you don't, just tap the edge of the knife into a block of wood with a stick or mallet (*not* a steel hammer! Brass is okay.) to hold it steady and then file away until the edges are sharp. You can further refine the back edges with a sharpening stone, but it really isn't necessary.

Axe sharpening is pretty much the same, except the angles are steeper and the bevel is established with a file. Wear a strong leather glove while doing this.

A bench-mounted belt sander with a new 80-grit belt is good for this too. It is quite easy to keep the steel cool with the belt sander. Do not use a powered bench grinder for this! Seriously! *Do not* do it. Those few who can do it without damaging the axe are experts and really don't need advice from this source.

After getting the angle right with the file or bench sander, use the stone to finish up the edge to get the burr, and so on, just like on the knife. But instead of moving the axe on the stone and strop, use the stone and strop on the stationary axe.

~ Sharpening ~

Make the axe shaving sharp, just like you would a knife.

The saws come really sharp and, avoiding dirt, can be kept sharp for a really long time. Replacement blades are available for the smaller saws, and the big ones can be sharpened by filing the tips of the teeth at the same angle that they came with.

The bent knife and gouge are just sharp edges with a curve. A little study and thought will reveal how that is done.

Always establish the correct angle, and get the burr, and then strop.

Always get the burr! Failure to get it while using the stone is the *main* reason people have trouble getting their tools sharp.

Saws are not stropped. Many people do not strop axes either. I do.

I strongly advise against loaning your knife or axe. People who do not have an axe or knife of their own usually have no idea how to use them, and as a result will almost inevitably damage them and/or themselves. I know this from experience! When someone asks, "Can I borrow your knife?," the correct and safest answer is: "What would you like *me* to cut for you?" You may have to further say, once that question is answered, "My knife does not get used for things like that. What you need is a crowbar!"

CHAPTER 3

~~~

Ways of Cutting

Please do not do bushcraft or any whittling or carving while wearing flip-flops. Good boots are best. Even when you are using a small knife, dropping it is a possibility—but when you are using axes especially, it is advisable to wear good, solid foot gear. Gloves are useful when breaking up wood and brush and working around the fire. Keep first-aid supplies close to hand.

A good and productive way of learning to whittle is just to make some shavings for starting a campfire. The project will be burned up but will have served a useful purpose.

For this, you need to prepare some sticks. Find some dry wood. Wood lying on the ground is often damp. If it hasn't been raining recently, it can be used once the fire is burning well, but it isn't much good for starting the fire. And learning to shave wood is a good start at doing something useful.

Dead standing trees that are not rotten can usually be found. Hit them with the back of an axe and it will be obvious which ones are sound, though dead, and which ones are rotten. Often the bark will be falling (or has already fallen) off the dead trunks or branches. The lower branches of evergreen trees are often dead, and if they snap off when pulled, they are dry. If they do not snap off, they are not dry—so move along.

Clumps of willows often have dead saplings that can be broken down by hand or easily cut down with the saw. Find sticks about 3" in diameter, then saw them into foot-long lengths.

Using the axe as shown below, split those little logs into sticks about 1" square. Notice that the axe is being "batoned." This is far better than batoning with a knife, though in a pinch that could be done.

~ Ways of Cutting ~

Axe use needs to be discussed. It is possible to get injured quite seriously with an axe. They have been used as weapons of war.

When—not *if*—your axe glances or misses, make sure it will not hit a foot or leg.

Pay attention. Careless axe use will result in serious injury.

Study the pictures. It is very advisable to get tutoring from an experienced axe user.

The hatchet, being smaller, needs special attention, because missing the branch or other target can easily result in a strike on the leg. When limbing, always keep the trunk of the tree between you and the hatchet or axe. Make sure there are no obstructions to swinging. Know where that axe head is going to wind up when it misses or glances. And it *will* miss and glance! Practice. A lot. Having an experienced axe user to observe and advise is very helpful. Yes, I said this already. So take note!

A CLOSE SHAVE

Now it's time to start shaving wood.

Sit as illustrated, working ahead of the knees. Do *not* even think of cutting down on your leg. Workbenches that bleed are no fun at all. It is almost impossible to bleed to death by cutting your hand, but if you cut the femoral artery in your leg, you have 10 minutes to live unless immediate action is taken. I have personally seen a moose killed by getting the femoral artery in its hind leg severed. Stay away from your legs with sharp things!

Hold the knife and the stick like this:

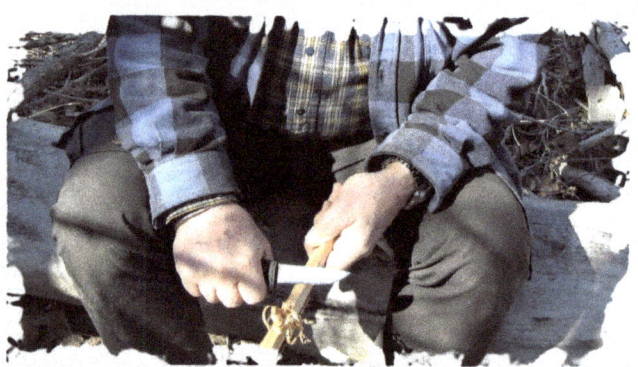

Take some shavings. Work on the corners of the stick. Make lots of shavings. And more shavings. Spend some time making big sticks into little ones, and produce a lot of shavings in the process.

~ Ways of Cutting ~

Try to make the shavings long and curly. Try to make some really tiny ones. Get a feel for the way the knife cuts and how the shavings can be curled.

Always cut in such a way that slipping—which *will* happen—will not result in injury.

While very useful, this first project won't last long. But it is a very important bushcraft skill to be able to split some dry wood and light a fire with a minimum of fuss.

Those shavings will light pretty easily with a match or lighter, and no paper or previously prepared firelighters will be needed.

DIFFERENT STROKES
There are many different ways to use the knife to cut. On the following pages, we'll look at some of the most useful for your purposes.

Here is a basic shaving stroke:

If you learn to slide the edge of the knife through the wood—that is, slice and apply pressure at the same time—cutting can be accomplished with a lot less pressure.

Using the basic cut, you can see how the edge first contacts the wood fairly close to the handle of the knife . . .

~ Ways of Cutting ~

. . . and slices through the wood, finishing up closer to the point of the knife at the end of the cut, as in the image below.

Here is another way to cut that is very precise. All the power for this cut comes from the thumb of the hand that is holding the stick. Practice this cut on a scrap stick. If there is follow through, you are doing it wrong. The whole point of this cut is to avoid follow-through.

STOP AND CONTROLLED CUTS

When wood is cut, because the knife is a wedge, a split develops ahead of the cutting edge. Knowing this allows you to use it to your advantage, with the following techniques.

If a stop cut is put across the grain first, with the knife or a saw, and a controlled cut like the thumb push is used, the split will be interrupted, or stopped, and the element that we don't want to cut will be preserved.

When making stop cuts, put the wood down on a firm surface, **not your leg!** A log or stump is good. The ground is not a good option.

A *controlled* cut is necessary for this to be effective. Uncontrolled cuts will just barrel through the stop cut.

Learn to use controlled cuts, as shown in the photo at the top of the facing page here.

The thumb push cut as explained above is a controlled cut. Use small cuts and deepen the stop cut as necessary until the desired depth is reached.

~ *Ways of Cutting* ~

Here is what can be done with stop and controlled clearing cuts.

Here is what I call the "potato peeler cut."

All the power for this cut comes from just closing the hand. Notice that the thumb is not in line with the blade.

PAY ATTENTION

Problems arise from this cut when whittlers try to make cuts that are too big and get their thumb lined up with the blade in an effort to put more power to it. Then when the wood suddenly yields, injury!

Here are a few of my watchwords:

Making big cuts is hopeless and dangerous.

Remember, *small* cuts.

Beginners have a fear of the blade. Get over it. The back of the blade will not hurt you.

~ Ways of Cutting ~

Here is how to grip the knife for the potato peeler cut. Notice that the blade is nestled in the first crease of the index finger.

Then when the hand is closed to make the cut, the thumb is naturally out of the way (as in the picture below).

Some people have trouble with this and just tend to nick their thumb. If this describes you, applying some tape to your thumb ahead of time might be useful. Duct tape, masking tape, hockey tape, or vet-wrap will all work. This is a very useful way of cutting and needs to be in the repertoire of every whittler, so learn it!

Cutting down on a piece of wood, a log, or a stump is always a good idea when possible. Cutting down on the ground is always a bad idea. Dull knives will result. Every time.

Under no circumstances cut down on your leg! If you do, you will remember this admonition in the emergency room.

Really make every effort to avoid emergency rooms! I have been in a few, but only once because of whittlin'. Other, more dangerous activities, like hockey, have taken me there on other occasions.

The one time I was there because of a whittlin' accident, I was making a carving mallet and shaving the handle with a knife that was bigger than I usually used. I dropped the mallet, foolishly tried to catch it with the hand that was holding the knife, and stabbed my hand. There's a lesson to be learned here: Let dropped whittlin's fall. Picking them up takes less time than bandaging, or getting stitches, which I got this time.

While the intern was stitching me up, she suddenly said "Oops." "Oops?" I replied. "You are not allowed to say oops! I thought they beat you in medical school if you say oops!" The supervising surgeon, a doctor whom I knew, said, "Yes, we will have to help her get over saying that!"

Keep your legs out of the action with cutting tools! Always be thinking, "What happens when this knife, axe, or chainsaw slips or bumps?" I know I keep saying this, but only because it is really important.

Here's another cut that will be very powerful and useful. It looks dangerous, but if done with the depicted hand positions and grips, the knife hand will make contact with the body before the blade does, making this quite safe. Study the pictures and make some non-cutting practice motions to confirm the safety of this before trying it for real.

Pinch the base of the blade or the handle of the knife right at the junction of handle and blade. Hold the pinch, and close the rest of the hand. Put the workpiece against the chest, keep the off hand behind the edge, and make a practice motion or two without cutting to confirm that the hand will hit the body before the blade can if the knife slips.

This is a very useful way of cutting when making treen. We will get there.

DRESS FOR SUCCESS

Using this cut will result in a sore chest, unless you are wearing thick winter clothing, or some other padding such as the shown wooden bib. It's called a "bodgers bib," and makes for a good and practical whittlin' project in its own right.

~ Ways of Cutting ~

Here is yet another very powerful way to cut.

Here the knife is held kind of backward, and both hands are held against the body. Then the blade is put on top of the wood to be cut, and the knife is levered in a backhanded motion.

The thumb of the off hand can be used to assist or to make this cut more precise.

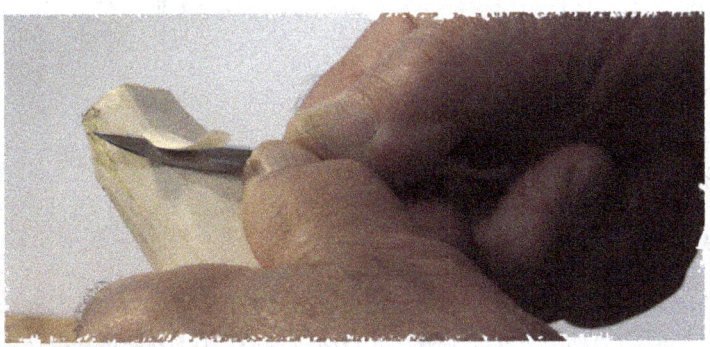

Only in serious emergencies, cut down on the ground or a rock. Doing so will damage the edge of your tool. Carving a spoon, for example, is not an emergency.

PUTTING IT ALL TOGETHER

OK. With some experience at cutting, you will be ready to do something with your ability.

Making really fine shavings like this will make ignition with a fire-steel, a ferrocerium rod, possible. Actually, if the shavings are fine enough, even green wood can be ignited with the fire-steel. In fact, I recommend it as good practice to learn to make green wood shavings so thin that they can be ignited with the fire-steel. Of course, to actually start a fire with green wood will require a lot of very fine shavings. If dry wood is available for the actual fire, there is no need to use green wood for the shavings, except to show off!

~ Ways of Cutting ~

If the forest is one that has a lot of pine, fir, or larch, it will be possible to harvest and use an absolutely reliable resource for fire starting, fatwood.

All that is necessary is some rotten pine, fir, or larch stumps or logs and an axe. The saw may help too. The stumps or logs should be falling apart rotten. Just tap them with the axe to see if they totally fall apart. If they do totally fall apart, there is no fatwood there. Move to another one.

If you encounter solid wood in a really rotten stump, that is likely resin-impregnated wood, or fatwood. Cut some out with the axe and if necessary the saw, and sniff. If it is fatwood, the turpentine smell will be obvious, and the glistening resin will be seen. This stuff will ignite even if it has been submerged. Split up a few pieces, some to make shavings and some to really get the fire going.

Here's an old rotten log that doesn't look like it is good for anything. But for a fatwood hunter, it is a gold mine!

See what was inside? Enough fatwood to light dozens of campfires!

Make some fine shavings and then some fuzzy scrapings, using the sharp corners on the back of the blade. These will ignite easily with the fire-steel or any other ignition source.

~ Ways of Cutting ~

Once a bushcrafter learns to find and use fatwood, he or she will never use anything else except for practice.

This stuff is far better than gasoline for lighting fires, for several reasons. First, it isn't dangerous. Gasoline is so dangerous that if it had been discovered in about 2001, none of us would be permitted to have it. A can of gas is more dangerous than a stick of dynamite without a blasting cap. People who light fires with gas will sooner or later burn themselves, because gasoline has fumes that will ignite.

Fatwood fumes will not ignite, but its shavings will, even if they have been submerged in water.

Unlike gasoline, fatwood does not need to be carried in a bottle or can. And if you know where to look, you will never need to buy it, although it is available for sale.

With a few fatwood shavings and a few small fatwood sticks, even damp firewood will ignite.

This all assumes a campfire is desired. Bushcrafting without a campfire is possible but weird.

Bushcrafters must observe rigorous safety procedures with fire, of course. Think about the weather, surroundings, and the potential for starting a forest fire.

~ *Ways of Cutting* ~

Gravel bars on rivers and pebbly or sandy shores of rivers and lakes, are good places to light fires. Rocks don't burn, unless they are coal—and finding some of that in a camping situation might be very handy.

I have a place on a stream where I like to fish. The creek is full of very hungry brook trout and some rainbows too. At this place out in the water is a big flat-topped rock. The water is only 6" or so deep on one side of the rock, and it makes a perfect place to light a fire and cook my fish. Absolutely, a safe place for a fire. I don't even need to bend over to tend the fire or look after the cooking. On the shore are some dead cottonwood trees with lots of fallen bark, which makes wonderful cooking coals. I can hardly wait to go there again!

The spot pictured below is another great place to fish. It's on the Ashnola River in southern British Columbia. No, I won't tell you where it is. I will take you there if you like!

Early in the season. Still a lot of snow around. The fish usually bite like crazy here. This day, not a nibble.

CHAPTER 4

~~~

Simple Disposable Items

Here are some suggestions for making and using a roasting stick, good for a hot dog, bratwurst, or marshmallows even.

Start the fire first. That will give it time to burn down to coals and enable roasting, not burning, the food. Might as well get the coffee water heating too. You likely will not burn that with hot flames.

CAMPFIRE COOKING

Find a live sapling about as thick as a thumb, or a little smaller. Taking one from a clump, or from the base of a larger tree, is not in any way desecrating the forest. It is just pruning a little. Avoid evergreens; they will impart flavors you will not enjoy. Maple, willow, alder, birch, ash, aspen, and cottonwood will all work for this. A dead branch will work but may ignite and even burn off while doing the roasting.

Find a stick that is as straight as possible, about 5' long, and with a fork, as shown on the next page. Remove the bark from the fork and point up the tines. It may be useful to thin the tines somewhat to avoid splitting the wiener or brat or whatever is being cooked.

A forked stick is preferable to a straight stick without a fork, because the food is more secure and can't twist on the stick.

I advise you figure out a support system for cooking with a forked stick: maybe some logs or rocks, even an available snowbank. If the ground is suitable, just sharpen the end of the roaster stick and push it in the ground.

Those who use their hands to hold the stick with the hot dog roasting on it often burn or undercook their food. Why? Simply because holding the stick becomes tedious.

Set up the stick so that the food is close enough to the coals to cook but not so close as to burn. Avoid cooking over flames. The fire can be kept flaming away from the food so it can continue to make coals or boil water for coffee.

Scrape some coals to one side to do the actual cooking. Test the distance from the coals by holding your hand over them. If you can barely hold your hand over the coals for a count of three, that should be about right.

Do not rush this. Cooked on the outside but not the middle is not desirable. Turn the food over after a while, and adjust the amount of coals as necessary, until the food is done. This

~ Simple Disposable Items ~

will take more than 10 minutes. Try to get out of the wind with your fire. The wind will mess up your cooking.

Now let's talk about roasting marshmallows. "I like mine burned" are the words of impatient people. I do not like mine burned.

Take your time. Look at the forked stick pictured below. See how it would be possible to put four marshmallows on it? Keep the whole deal far enough from the coals, not flames, so that they will heat all the way through with nice browning on the outside until they will almost fall off the stick from their own weight. Perfect!

Now that we've mastered the simple roasting stick, let's take a look at making dingle sticks and pot hooks.

A dingle stick is used to dangle pots over a fire. People often make these out of sticks that are too thin and short. But if the dingle stick is hefty and long enough, it can be arranged to be more stable. A dead sapling can be used for this.

The pot can be hung directly on the stick, but it is more efficient to make a couple of pot hooks that will allow you to more easily adjust the height of the pot over the flames. Pot hooks also make is easier to take the pot off the heat, or to put it back on. To make a pot hook, use a green forked stick as shown below.

~ Simple Disposable Items ~

Cut an X with the saw, on the same side of the stick as the branch.

A knife can be used for this, or even an axe in the hands of someone with some practice, but it's easiest with the saw. Put the end of the pot hook on a log or stump—*not the ground*—to whittle out the notch. If the blade contacts the ground, it will be dulled. Every time. Zero exceptions.

This might look like a precarious setup for hanging the pot, yet it is quite secure unless someone kicks the dingle stick!

Always back up the cuts with clean wood. Use lots of small cuts rather than a few big ones, so as to not split off the end of the pot hook. If the pot has a fairly large handle, more than one notch can be made to facilitate height adjustments. Keep in mind, there needs to be clearance for the lid of the pot, if there is one. Two or three pot hooks of various lengths can be made for adjusting the height of the pot too.

~ Simple Disposable Items ~

Here's another style of dingle stick and pot hook. It takes a little longer to make, but it is easier to adjust.

Pot hooks make adjusting and adding/removing pots from the fire very easy. Try both styles and see which one you like.

There are other, two-piece pot hooks that I guess are kind of fun to make and have the appearance of being more secure, but I have never experienced a problem with the above styles and do not consider the two-piece ones to be worth the effort.

Once you've got your cooking setup, a stirring implement will come in handy. This stirring stick for soup or porridge, often called a spurtle, is very easy to make. Any old piece of wood will suffice. Just whittle off the bark and any splinters, and stir away!

Taking off the bark is an obvious precaution, as it will have dirt and maybe even living things on it! The bare wood underneath will be clean. After use, just whittle the last meal off the spurtle and—bingo!—it's clean again.

Spurtles can be flattened to be more like a spatula, as show here, which may make them even more useful.

~ Simple Disposable Items ~

NO NEED FOR SILVERWARE!

Small forked branches are easy to make into, well, forks! Just find some branches of the size needed, whittle off the bark, and sharpen the tips.

Round out your tableware with a spreader—a simple tool that's like a little wooden knife. Spreaders can be as simple as a slightly flattened stick, as pictured below, or very intricate (certainly something that wouldn't just be tossed in the fire when it is time to go home).

PITCH A BUSHCRAFT TENT

Tent pegs are so easy to make that it seems silly to bring plastic ones. This is especially true because in some kinds of ground, the plastic ones are just too small.

Here are a couple of ways to make them.

in the first option, a piece of firewood can be split down, sharpened, and notched pretty quickly. Sturdier pegs like the one demonstrated below are particularly useful when the ground is kind of sandy and a small peg just won't hold, or in situations where a larger tarp needs to be kept secure when there is some wind.

Make them as big as needed for the ground type, weather conditions, and tent/tarp size. This is a great project for axe whittlin'.

If you're just looking to replace those plastic ones, or to supplement them, cut some live saplings about 1" in diameter, with little branches that can keep the tent loops or ropes from slipping off. Make them long enough to be secure.

~ *Simple Disposable Items* ~

The folding saw, axe, and knife can be used to make a lot of tent pegs quite quickly.

These whittlin' projects do not require a lot of expertise or even practice to accomplish effectively. They can function quite well even if they are pretty crude, but they are very helpful around the campsite and can serve as an introduction to projects requiring more finesse.

CHAPTER 5

~~~

Treen

Treen refers to utilitarian items made from wood. Literally, from "the tree." Treen is usually made from green material directly from the tree. Most treen items are tools to help with cooking and serving food.

Again, these items can be quite crude and still work very nicely. However, with practice and attention to detail, treen can become objects of art. The focus of this chapter will be to go beyond the crude, and learn to make items that are not only useful but also visually pleasing.

A good place to start with treen is to source good wood. Avoid conifer and evergreen wood. It is possible to make treen out of it, but pine, spruce, and fir are resinous and will impart flavors to food that most people find objectionable. So focus on deciduous tees, those that have leaves, not needles. Avoid really hard woods too. Oak, apple, and hard maple are difficult for whittlers to work.

If you do not have access to public forests, you can contact tree services in your community. These people trim and remove problem trees and usually really know wood. They are often quite cooperative when asked for wood by whittlers. Cultivate these people! I have found that they like the idea that at least a little of the wood that they cut will be used for something other than burning.

Construction lumber will drive you nuts for carving treen, and it would definitely not fit in with the idea of bushcraft whittlin' anyway.

CHOOSING THE RIGHT WOOD

My favorite wood for treen, birch, is the one that has a long tradition of being used for such crafts in the lands long associated with this work. Scandinavia, Russia, and northern North America are all popular areas for treen. I recommend using birch if you can get it. The softer varieties of maple work well. Douglas maple and bigleaf maple are two that I have used with success. I am sure there are other varieties.

Alder has wide distribution in North America and can be used for treen. I have used alder in northern British Columbia and in Southern California. One advantage to alder is that while some people might object to the cutting of a birch, almost no one cares if some smallish alders are cut out of a thicket.

I do not like basswood for treen. It is easy to carve, but spoons and ladles made out of it need to be pretty clunky to be strong enough to use. Basswood does not grow wild in my part of the country, but it might in yours, and it is great for a lot of whittlin' projects.

It comes down to using what is available.

Pay attention when traveling the backroads and trails. Often land is being cleared, or trees have fallen down, or roads are being constructed, and lots of wood is available for the asking, or just for the picking up. Be aware that if it is birch that is being considered, it needs to be processed within a month or so of coming down in warm weather and shortly after frost is no longer common in the spring if it came down or was cut down in the winter. Birch bark is waterproof, so the wood within starts to rot fast if the bark is left on, even while the bark makes it look just fine. A birch log cut in June will be unusable in September, unless the bark has been removed and the wood split down the middle. Attempting to fudge on this will always result in disappointment if functional wooden spoons and such are the goal.

Large logs, 12" in diameter, can certainly be used for making treen, but unless larger bowls are the project, they are not necessary. Good spoons, ladles, and spatulas can be made out of trees 3" to 4" diameter.

I went out looking for birch early in the spring, and there it was! A birch that had been taken down by the snow, I guess. This area had a lot of snow at that elevation that year. At least four feet. It was down but very fresh.

Let's start with the simplest project, a spatula, which is a very useful tool at the campsite or in the kitchen.

Start with a little log, say, 3½" diameter and about 15" long. It is best if the wood is quite fresh. The very best is if it has been cut in the last five minutes. The last two days is OK too. If the wood has been down for a while, cut off the end well past any cracks in the end of the piece, then measure approximately 15" and cut it off the larger pole.

Using the hatchet, or axe as shown, split the little log right down the middle. The best way to do this without wasting wood by making inaccurate cuts is to start a split with the axe. This is most accurately done by tapping the axe with a hefty stick—not another axe! This may be enough to split the piece in half.

~ Treen ~

If necessary, a couple of wedges can quickly be made and used to do the splitting.

Here's a little bent log I found that will facilitate the making of a spatula with a curve to it. Spoonmakers call this a "crank."

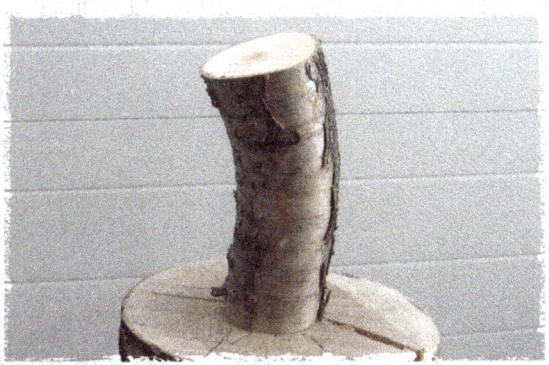

I split it with my little pack axe/hatchet.

By the way, it's best if there are no branches on a log like this, because they will produce knots. If branches are unavoidable, try to split the log in such a way that the part that you will use for the project will not have any of the knots.

As mentioned before, do not do any of this axe work on the ground. Always use a chopping block or the flattened side of a large log. Even a plank on the ground will work. If logs are split while one end is on the ground, grit will be pounded into the log and that will dull tools as additional work is done. Also, it is easy to hit the ground with the axe, which will dull it. Be paranoid about keeping your edges sharp. It will save a lot of time and you will do better work. (And remember, do not loan your sharp tools if you want them to stay sharp!)

Now we are going to "hew," which is the correct word for axe whittlin'. Flatten the part of the log that was the center of the tree and remove *all* traces of the very center of the tree, the pith. If this is not removed, cracks will form as the wood dries.

This is done by scoring the wood with the axe as shown and then hewing the wood away between the scoring marks. Scoring could be done with the saw too.

Now score and hew the other side of the log half, until a little board of an even thickness of about 1" to 1½" has been produced, as shown. Square up the edges.

Now the shape of the project can be sketched on the board, top and side views. Do the sketching. It will make the project much easier. Once you have done a lot of this sort of thing, you may well dispense with sketching, but at first it will help quite a lot. You might want to strive for symmetry. Or not. Either way will result in a functional tool.

Now use the saw to put some stop cuts on the project, to help prevent splitting into or off parts that you want to keep on the project.

Real experts do not need these stop cuts, or might make them with their axe. Scoring, as mentioned earlier, is just creating stop cuts with the axe. When you're starting out, it will be a lot easier to get good results if you make them with your saw.

If enough of these sawn stop cuts were put into the blank, the rest of the shaping could be done with a knife. The more there are, the less pressure needs to be applied, hence less likelihood of error.

Hew out the pattern as close as possible with the axe.

Then use whatever knife blade works to refine the shape. Thin the front edge to facilitate flipping eggs and such. Round the edges of the handle to make it more comfortable to use. I find that spoons and spatulas with flattish handles are easier to hold and use.

Make sure that enough wood is left in this area. Made like this, the spatula will be strong enough to use, but not clunky.

Put it to work.

If you want to make a fork, just make a spatula and then cut two slots with the saw to set yourself up for whittling a fork with three tines.

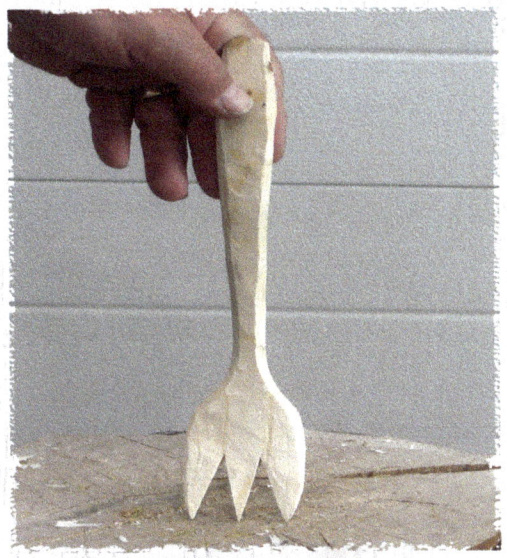

Now let's make the classic treen project now: a wooden spoon or a ladle.

Most beginner spoon carvers make ladles, not spoons. Ladles have deeper bowls. Spoons are quite shallow and are *very* shallow, if well designed and executed, at the front end. This means that they will be stronger and less prone to chipping at that front end. Because spoons are general-use instruments, they need to be strong for stirring, scraping, and so on. Ladles are helpful in serving soup, stew, and similar things.

There is no reason not to whittle ladles as well as spoons, but my suggestion is to do a spoon or two first and then make some ladles.

That said, the pictures to follow show a ladle being made, using a bent tree that just begged to be made into a ladle.

At first, go at this just like you did with the spatula. Just leave a little more thickness in the little board that is hewn out of the log.

Sketch out the shape and top and side views, remembering that spoons and ladles, unlike spatulas, have a shallow bowl, so allow sufficient material for this.

Notice the wood that is left on ahead of the spoon bowl. This is left there to take the brunt of the pounding that occurs during hewing, so that cracks do not form in the area that will become the bowl. It will be sawn off later.

~ *Bushcraft Whittling* ~

~ Treen ~

After hewing and whittling the top- and side-view shape, draw out the inside edge of the spoon bowl with a pencil.

Now using the gouge or the bent knife, scoop out the bowl, carving *across* the grain as much as possible.

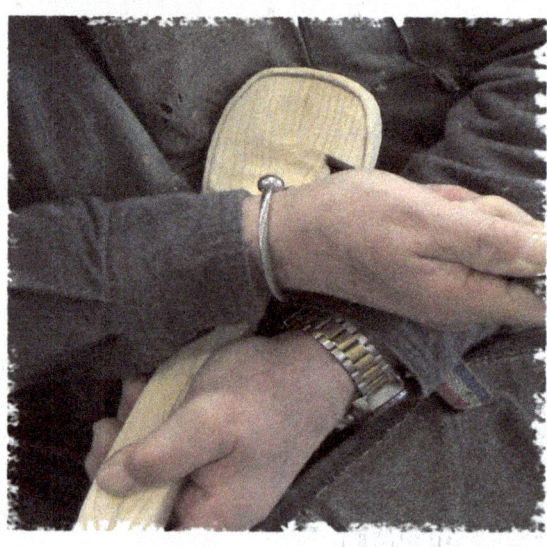

~ Treen ~

It is a really good idea to practice this whittlin' technique for a while on scrap wood before actually trying it on your real spoon or ladle.

Trust me on this—those who ignore this advice will soon wish they hadn't.

Do not get too deep at the front end. Most people do. Do not be one of "those" people!

A ladle will be deeper than a spoon. But even so, if the bowl is deep and steep at the front end, it will be weak and prone to chipping. Take it easy. Many small cuts. After a lot of spoons, confidence will allow greater speed. A little from one direction, and then from the other.

Once the inside of the bowl is formed, it is time to shape the outside, as shown on the next page. If you're going to use the axe for some of this, the wisdom of that extension we noted earlier will be very obvious. When the axe use is all done, the extension can be carefully sawn off. The knife or knives can do the rest. Again, use small cuts—and watch the grain.

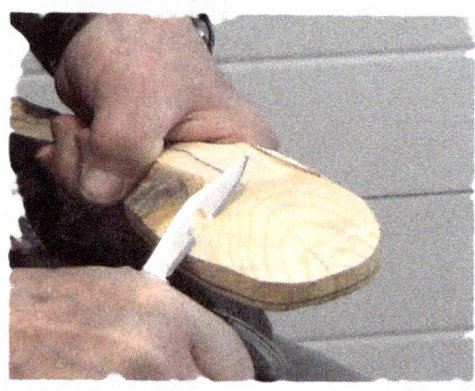

Strive for a light, non-clunky but strong spoon or ladle. The joint of the handle and bowl is very important. The following shapes can accomplish light and strong. Other shapes, not so much.

Flat handles on spoons are easier to use.

Finish the edge of the bowl carefully. Mixing and serving spoons will benefit from a sharp edge. Smaller eating spoons are better with rounded edges.

Get creative, but keep the basic strength and utility of the spoon or ladle in mind.

There are people who have just gone nuts on this whole spoon-whittlin' thing! Spoon-carving festivals are held in various places in North America, Britain, and possibly other places, where hundreds of people gather to share ideas and wood and make lots of very nice spoons.

It is kind of addictive. So be warned. You might not be able to stop!

CHAPTER 6

~~~

Walking Sticks, Canes, and Crutches

Over 30 years ago, I was on a backpacking trip with a few other guys in the eastern foothills of the Rocky Mountains, about 65 miles south of Dawson Creek, British Columbia (Mile Zero of the Alaska Highway). One of the group developed a knee problem when we were still a two-day hike from our vehicles. I made a walking stick for him that enabled him to walk out and saved the rest of us from having to carry him, though we did carry some of his gear. He still has that stick.

WALKING TALL

Beyond being useful in an emergency, walking sticks are helpful for almost anyone while negotiating rough terrain. Plus, they can be a medium of artistic expression, and therefore are worthy projects for the bushcraft whittler.

Let's start with a simple, made-in-the-boonies walking stick that a hiker may make, use, and then discard before heading home.

This is a very simple procedure. Many people have just picked up a dead stick and used that, sometimes for years!

Here are a few suggestions that I think will help in coming up with a functional walking stick.

Sometimes a dead stick can be found that will serve the purpose, but mostly a live sapling will be stronger, more flexible, and therefore less likely to disappoint the hiker by breaking at an inopportune moment. While it is neither advisable nor permitted for bushcrafters to harvest live wood in a park or some similar setting, taking some saplings out of a tight thicket or suckers from the base of a tree is not in any way harming the forest. Those who maintain orchards annually cut enormous amounts of wood from their trees to make the entire orchard healthier. Also, the areas alongside roads—sometimes called "the road allowance"—often produce a lot of saplings that will get trimmed out by those who maintain those roads. Stick makers often consider these places as "walking stick ranches!"

A couple of basic walking sticks:

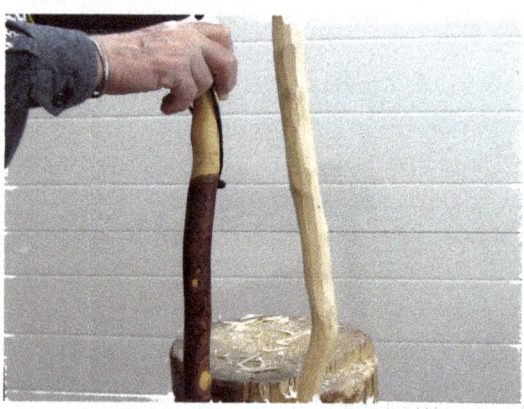

START WITH THE RIGHT STICK

Choose a stick that will be strong enough, and light enough, and easy enough to work. Some species of wood can be quite strong even if the wood is slender, while others may need a little more thickness but may be easier to work and get quite light when the wood dries out. If a stick is needed immediately, it comes down to a matter of using what is available.

Avoid evergreens if possible. They usually have a lot of pitch and will be, well, *sticky*.

Choose a straight stick long enough to be a help. The rougher the terrain, the longer the stick that is needed. For hiking very gentle hills or flat ground, hip height will work. For fording streams/rivers, very steep hills, big rocks and logs, and so on, a shoulder-height stick or even longer is required. In really extreme situations, two sticks will make even scary situations quite negotiable.

A REAL-WORLD EXAMPLE

Once in the Arizona desert, I climbed up into a basin where there was a spring. That spring, as it would happen, was the reason that the nearby Yuma prison, many years ago, operated a granite-quarrying operation down below the basin, working on the automobile-size boulders that were and are very common in the area. The water meant that they could live and work there.

Anyway, when it was time to climb down out of the basin, I became quite concerned that going down was going to be a lot harder and more hazardous than climbing up because of the huge boulders. I needed a walking stick. Really I needed two sticks. No suitable trees were around, but there were dead stalks of a yucca-type plant, locally known as the century plant. They are not wood, but they do make good, light walking sticks. I cut two of them about 7' long, and they did the trick! It was kind of fun hopping down the rocky ravine from boulder to boulder with the help of my two sticks and I am sure it took less than half the time that it would have taken without them.

Use the stick with the big end up. It will be much more comfortable. Try it with the big end down and you will find out why.

Carefully cut the sapling down in such a way that it won't get all cracked up and ragged in the process. Sometimes, if the piece has fairly smooth bark, it can be left on. Usually I find it better to shave off the bark and a little of the underlying wood. This speeds the drying process, and that will make the stick a lot lighter. Rough bark can be hard on the hands.

I usually start working on the small end of the stick first, tucking it under my arm, or working down on a log or clean stump, until I have whittled about a foot of the stick. Now I can brace the stick against the ground to whittle the rest of it with no danger of hitting the ground and dulling my knife. And if that small end gets gritty, it's okay, I don't need to cut it any more anyway.

Smooth off any knots or small branches, and round off the sharp corners on the ends. To trim knots, first use the axe and then clean up with the knife. Keep the stick between you and the tool; that way any slips will not result in injury. Use many small cuts with the knife. Do not attempt big ones; they will produce frustration.

Also, cutting toward the center of the knot, first from one side and then the other, will reduce tear-out.

While working on one end, if the other end gets jammed into the ground and gets all gritty, take the time to clean off that gritty end by sawing off about a half inch. This way, you will not dull your knife.

The stick can be personalized by whittling your initials in it, or carving a wood spirit, a caricature head, an animal head, or maybe a stylized eagle. More on this later.

Walking sticks can be used before they are completed. Once they are cut to length, they can be a work in progress that is continued as time permits, and can be fully functional during that process.

To make a cane, a little more diligence in finding the right branch will be required. Birches and other trees often fall, or they are knocked over but continue to grow. The branches that grow at right angles to the fallen trunk can be cut with the saw and axe to make good canes.

One day I was having trouble finding branches growing at right angles until I found this one. If used in the traditional cane way, it is awkward, but if used this other way, it is quite comfortable. It may be even better than the traditional style of cane.

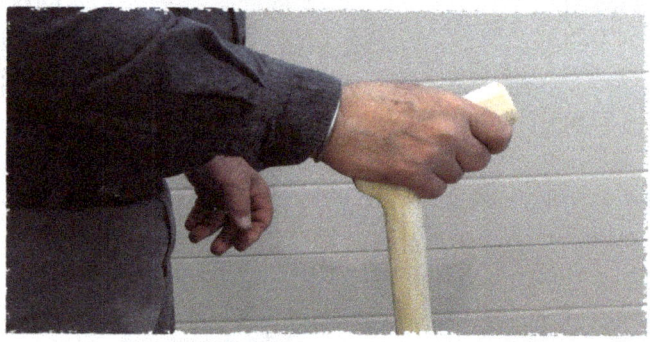

If someone needs a crutch, even more ingenuity and perseverance will be required to find the right branch. I found this one, and the pictures show my progress in making the crutch.

~ Walking Sticks, Canes, and Crutches ~

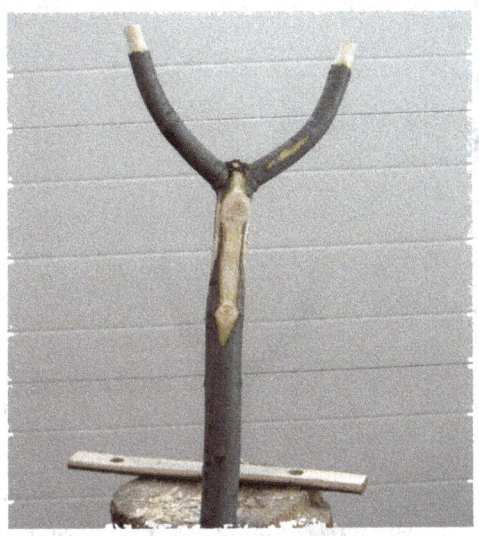

You'll need holes in the cross piece so it can fit onto the fork, and a brace-and-bit type of auger is *very* useful for drilling holes out in the boonies. This is a cordless drill, kids! Never needs recharging either. These things can often be found at flea markets and secondhand stores. Fifty years ago and more they were very common. Now many people do not even know what they are for.

The small blade of the pocketknife could also be used to whittle out the necessary holes in the cross piece. Do not stab the knife in and twist to attempt to drill a hole. It won't work and is dangerous. Just cut a little at a time until the hole is made.

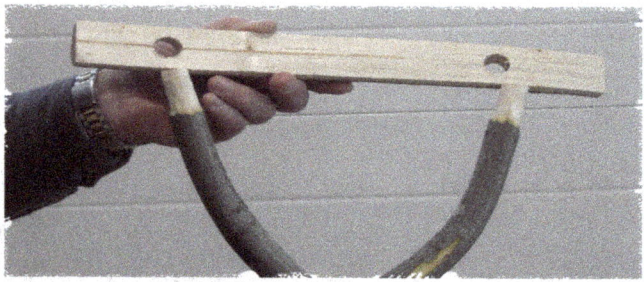

After the crosspiece fits down on the fork—it doesn't have to be supertight—cut slots in the ends of the fork so that little wedges can be tapped in to make the whole thing tight. Notice the orientation of the wedges in relation to the crosspiece. If the slots and wedges line up with the grain of the crosspiece, it will split when the wedges are tapped in. Always put wedges into tenons (the parts that poke into the holes) *across* the grain of the mortises (the holes).

There. This will work. Of course it will be necessary to cut it to the right length.

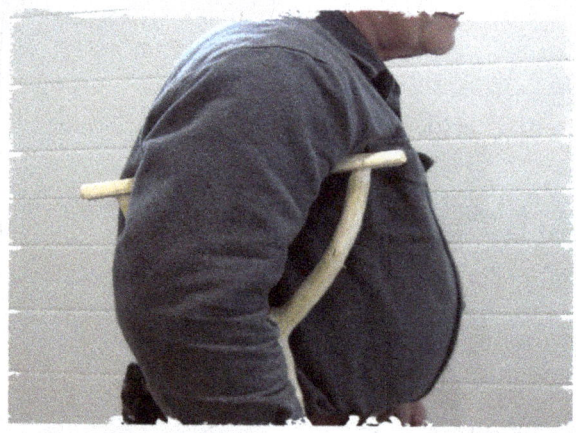

If it is ever necessary to splint a broken arm or leg, the forest will provide. A couple of saplings smoothed down and cut to length will do the job. Nothing too intricate here. Just clean things up so that the splints do not cause further injury or irritation and tie them on, preferably with cloth strips or bandannas. The idea is to keep the limb from moving, and whatever will accomplish that will work.

I once encountered a very serious motor vehicle accident with seven or eight victims. There was one fatality and one unconscious person. I helped splint some injured arms. It took well over an hour for an ambulance to arrive at the scene.

Some very experienced medical people were there though, and they instructed us to use magazines to splint injured arms. When I was a first-aid attendant in a factory, we were trained to use aluminum mesh for splints. Saplings work too.

CHAPTER 7

~~~

Walking Sticks with Personality

Here is how to carve a wood spirit into your stick and give it some "style."

Choose a stick that is thick enough so that it will still be strong enough to be used after carving the wood spirit. It is better to have a stick that is too thick to begin with. Just shave it down after the face carving.

You can see that the stick here in my left hand is what I would consider to be too thin to do a wood spirit in. It could be done, but the carving will be very small and fiddly.

Choose an area on the stick that does not have knots and is not where the user will grab it when walking.

Draw a vertical line on the bark. That will be the center line for the face. Whittle off two flat planes that intersect at that center line, forming a 90-degree angle with it. Do not fudge on this! Most beginner problems in carving wood spirits are traceable to the failure to do this important basic act!

Sketch on the hairline as shown and take off a wedge of wood, as seen below, which will form the top of the nose and the forehead.

Mark and cut a little brow notch and two stop cuts across the little corners as shown. Cut up and down, removing the little corners to form the sides of the nose and the eye sockets.

Now mark and then whittle clearing cuts—using a stop cut and thumb push cuts—to remove some material under the nose. Make sure you make good stop cuts. The use of thumb push cuts is important here, because without the control provided by them there is a high probability of cutting off the nose, which is undesirable. Do not go deeper into the wood under the nose than above it.

Draw in the hair as it frames the face, and the mustache. Remember, a pencil is your inexpensive and very helpful friend in all of this. Use it.

Mark in the width of the nose too, as shown. Noses have a way of getting smaller as we whittle. Start with one that is quite large, and the results will be better. Even if the finished project has a big nose, it will look better than a tiny one.

OK. Follow the pictures, putting in stop cuts and clearing out material to form the facial features.

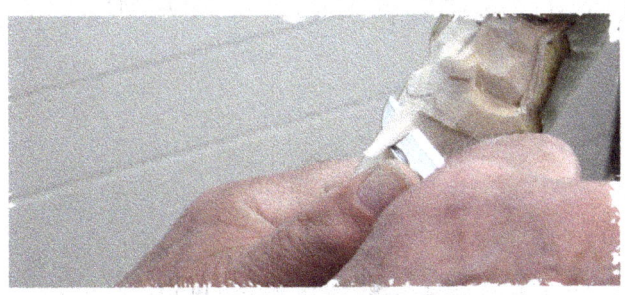

For eyes, just cut in some thin slits along the same stop cut line that was originally made when making the two open notches for the eye sockets.

Be safe! Do not put the project on your leg as you cut. Keep the hand not holding the knife in a safe position so that when the knife slips, no blood is extracted! Make lots of small cuts. Avoid big ones.

~ Bushcraft Whittling ~

Here's the finished product:

AN AMERICAN CLASSIC

How about an eagle stick?

I saw an article in *Woodcarving Illustrated* magazine a couple of years ago where the author had adapted some designs of the renowned John Bellamy, who developed and carved some wonderful eagle carvings at the end of the 19th century in New England. Eagles done like his have become known as "Bellamy Eagles." This author showed how to carve an eagle stick, with a kind of Bellamy eagle on it. He used a glued-up basswood blank, which he then roughed out with a band saw. I have, in turn, adapted his idea, and done it on natural sticks without roughing out with the band saw.

I strongly recommend that inexperienced whittlers, before making a stick like this, get a chunk of cottonwood bark, which is easy to whittle, or maybe a piece of the same wood that will be used to make the stick, and make a practice piece. Make your mistakes—and there will be some—on the practice piece, not on the one you want to keep and use.

Start with a stick like this:

It may take a little hunting to find one like this, but they are out there. This one is Douglas maple, a bush, rarely a tree, that grows in my area. Birch would have been good too, or willow. Use what you can find as long as it isn't too hard. If the wood is alive when you cut it, you will find it easier to carve while it is still wet.

Using an axe or hatchet, flatten the sides of the end that will become the head of the eagle, as shown. It needs to be tapered down quite a lot.

~ *Walking Sticks with Personality* ~

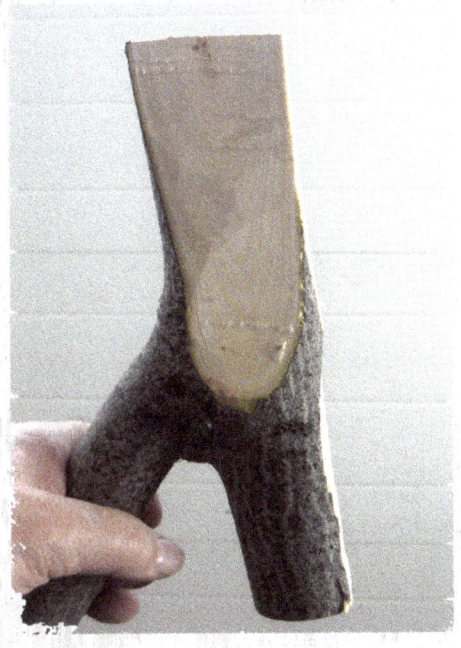

Sketch the profile of the eagle. I used a felt-tipped pen to make it easier to see in the photos, but a pencil will work fine. Use your pencil a lot when whittlin' figures. You don't have to make elaborate drawings, but a few marks will help keep things on track. In fact, really good drawings can be a problem, because after drawing really nice pictures on a piece of wood, many whittlers are reluctant to cut them off.

My drawings are pretty pathetic, and I can't wait to cut them off! They *have* to be cut off. Then they can be redrawn where necessary.

Use the saw to help get a start on shaping the profile, and maybe even the axe, and then use your pocketknife. Use whatever blade will do the best job. Having a three-bladed pocketknife means that there are three knives in one package. Sometimes you will need a longer blade, sometimes you will want one with a straight edge. Experiment. Don't get locked in trying to do it all with one blade.

Use the photos for reference and shape the eagle's head and beak. Notice how the beak is thinner toward the tip. Don't make it fragile though!

This straight-on view, in the photo below, gives you a good guideline for a thickness that works artistically and functionally.

~ Walking Sticks with Personality ~

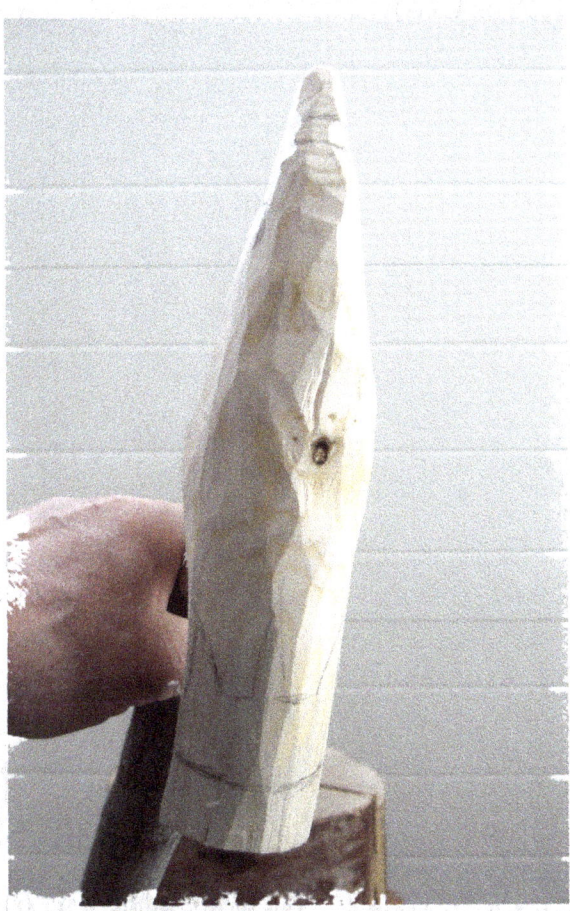

Give the bird a very pronounced brow above his eyes. Eagles have the appearance of being perpetually annoyed, and the heavy brow will help with that look.

So make a good stop cut under the brow and then at the base of the beak, and then clear out some material under the brow, which will become the eye area. By the way, that raised part at the base of the beak is called the cere, and our Bellamy eagle example is radically stylized, as is the beak.

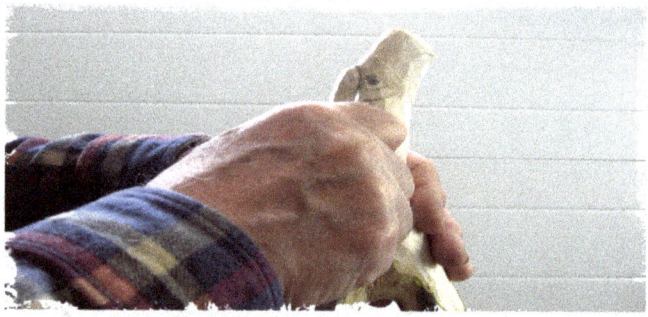

Draw in the eye with a semicircle as shown. Use stop cuts and clearing cuts to carefully round it up a bit. Then make a little groove for the iris and a divot for the pupil.

~ Walking Sticks with Personality ~

Save the rest of the carving of the beak for later.

Sketch in the wings and tail in whatever proportions seem pleasing to you. Remember, it is stylized, so you can use the wonderful freedom afforded by "artistic license."

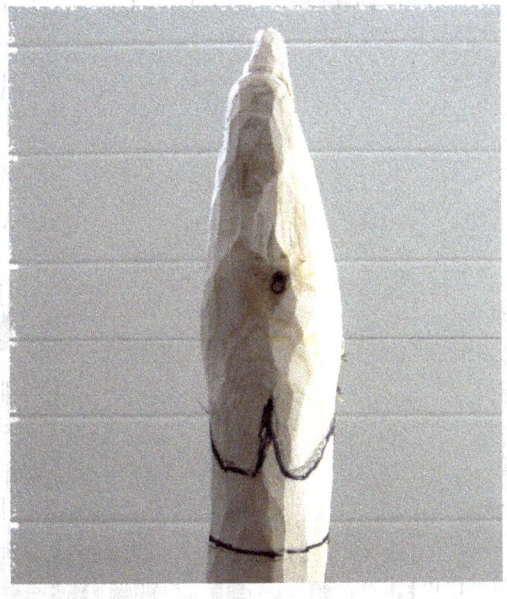

~ Bushcraft Whittling ~

Again, using stop cuts and clearing cuts, make the wings stand out a bit and lower the tail. Then put in a few wing and tail feathers.

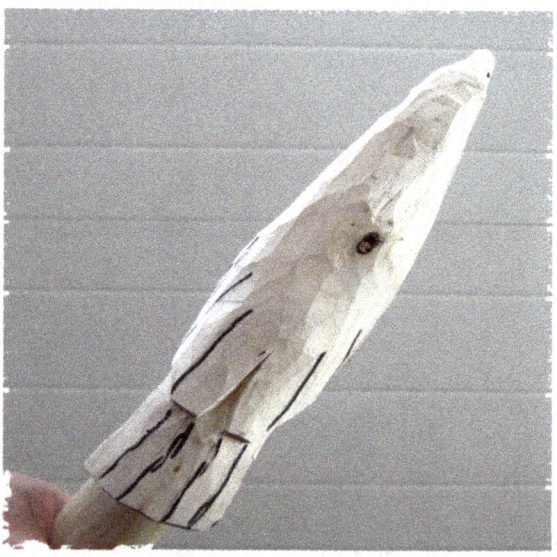

~ Walking Sticks with Personality ~

Very carefully carve out the rest of the beak. **No prying! Small cuts.** It looks good to get right through as shown, but avoid getting things so thin that it gets fragile. It is a walking stick and will get knocked around.

This particular stick is about the right diameter for a walking stick, so I just needed to shave off the bark and scrape off the inner bark using the back of my folding saw. If your stick is thicker, you may want to whittle it down some.

There. A pretty unique and distinctive walking stick.

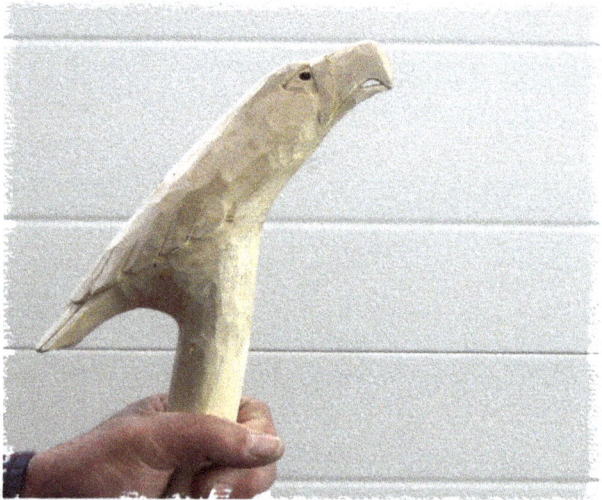

Whittle walking sticks down so that they aren't clunky. I have seen some that made me think that the user might get arrested for illegal logging!

~ *Walking Sticks with Personality* ~

A REAL CHARACTER!

This is kind of a progression of the wood spirit idea. Again, I suggest making a practice piece first.

Here is a cottonwood bark model of what I will carve on a walking stick. I carved teeth on the model (just couldn't resist!) but didn't on the stick. You might notice other differences.

This stick was a little bit larger than 2" in diameter at the big end. Remember, we always put the big end up in making and using walking sticks. Aspen, or "white poplar" as some people call it, is the wood. Lots of other kinds of wood are fine for this, but again, avoid the needle trees and really hard woods like hickory or oak. Aspen is quite easy to carve, especially when green, and gets very light when it dries out. Birch, alder, and willow are good for this too.

~ *Walking Sticks with Personality* ~

This guy is going to have a top hat, so after drawing in the center line of his face, I sketched in the underside of the hat brim. That center line will be the middle of his face, and that needs to be knot free. There is a knot a little farther down on this stick, but it won't be a problem there.

Under the hat brim, whittle off two flat planes that intersect at about a 90-degree angle right on the center line. Leave the line on for now.

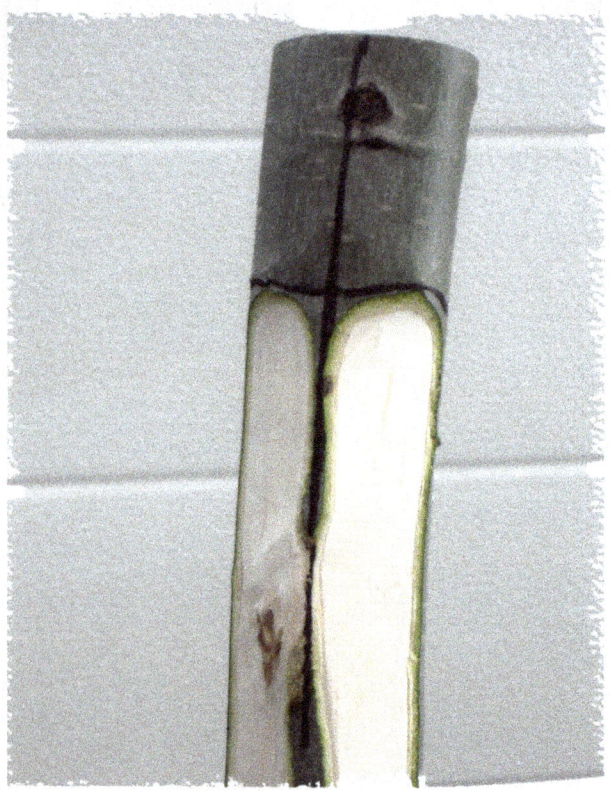

It is absolutely essential that these two flat planes be whittled on any surface upon which a human face will be whittled, whatever the final object might be.

If this is not done, the result usually is a flat face. This absolutely drives me nuts because it is so easy to avoid. So help me with my mental health and do it right!

Then make a stop cut all the way around the hat brim. Use thumb push cuts so as not to cut unduly into the hat brim, which would make it fall off. Later, extend the two flat planes right up to the hat, and make a notch, as shown, all the way around the back of the head.

Study the next photos. Take out a triangle of wood as shown. Pay attention to the proportions here. If the notch is too big, the face will have an enormous nose, which you may like. I like big noses on my faces, but not *that* big.

About halfway down on that notch, make a little mark and then two lines that extend with a tiny droop right over the corners of the notch. These will become the lower lids of the eyes. If the lines do not have any droop, the figure will look "wooden."

"No kidding," you say. We are making a wood figure here but do not want him to look "wooden," which is to say lifeless or without any personality.

That said, getting the expression you want is also an important thing to keep, as it were, an eye on.

If the lines droop a lot, our guy will look tired or sad. If we angle them up, he will look angry, or even deranged! Watch out! Little things can have drastic consequences!

The circles on this photo are not eyes but are there to show where wood will be removed to make the eye sockets and the side of the nose.

In order to carve those sockets the way you'll want them in order to set your face up for the finer details, follow the instructions on the following pages.

First make a stop cut right on the line, and then, using careful thumb push cuts, make these two even, wide notches that will become the eye sockets and the sides of the nose.

~ Walking Sticks with Personality ~

Here is where we are now:

A little ways down from the start of the wedge, mark the underside of the nose and sketch in the hairline. Notice that this line is not straight up and down but is drawn so that the face is narrower at the forehead than at the cheeks.

Also notice that the hair extends below the level of the nose so as to cover the area that would have ears. Ears are fragile on walking sticks and difficult to carve, so I am suggesting that you avoid them by hiding them under the hair.

Put a stop cut at the underside of the nose, and using thumb push cuts *only*, clear out the area under the nose. It is vitally important that you use thumb push cuts here! If you do not, you *will* regret it because you will cut or split off that nose and need to start over. Also, be sure that you do not get under your stop cuts, because that will result in the same disastrous effect. Do not go deeper into the stick under the nose than you did up under the hat brim. If you do, your figure will have a weird overbite or other orthodontic issues.

~ Walking Sticks with Personality ~

See how the stop cut is put in along the hairline at the sides of the face and then the material is cleared out to form the temples. Keep your non-cutting hand in a safe place at all times. It is easy to forget and then bleed. Watch the grain in all of this, and take care to not make the forehead wider than the temples. Study the pictures and make yours like mine and you'll be okay.

Next, you'll want to make a notch as shown under the hair all around the back, as shown in the photo below, carefully following along the line you've already established.

Now you're ready to return to your character's face and begin refining the important details that will give him his character.

Notice in the photos here that a couple of cuts have been made so that the center of the nose on the underside, the septum, is lower than the outside of the nostrils. Also round off the end of the nose.

Notice also that I have trimmed the hair down where it disappears under the hat to reflect the fact that when the hat is placed on the head, the hair is mashed right down to nothing.

Put a stop cut at the widest part of the nose on each side. Notice that the nose is *not* undercut and that the stop cut is at an angle. Always make noses bigger than you think they should be. They will get smaller as you work, and if they start out small, they will be really tiny by the time you finish.

~ Walking Sticks with Personality ~

Now, once you've got the basic shape roughed in, it's time to clean out the area beside the nose. Aren't you glad you left yourself a little room for error?

Define the nose a little using a rolling kind of a cut. *Do not* run a stop cut all the way up the side of the nose. Go look in a mirror. Without ever having met you, I can say with almost total certainty that except for the area immediately adjacent to your nostrils, the junction between your nose and cheek is not a sharp line but is softly curved. Look at the photos. See how there is a soft junction between the nose and cheek.

Make that lump of wood that occupies the nose position actually look like a nose. Study the pictures. Look in the mirror. Cut carefully. When cutting features like the inside of the nostrils, *always* cut from the outside toward the inside, from the weakest part toward the strongest. If you start at the septum of the nose, for example, and try to cut toward the outside of the nose, you will crack that entire nostril off! I know you do not want to do that. So cut from the outside of the nose toward the center.

It is time to sketch the mustache in, with nice curves for the top and just a straight line, for now, for the bottom.

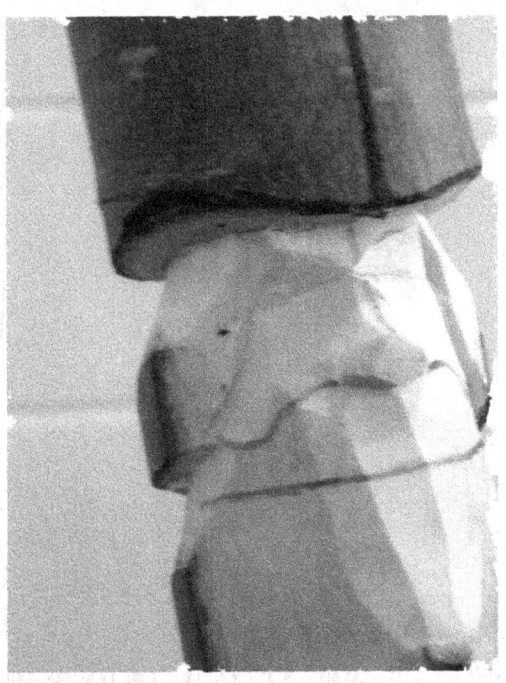

I am making that mustache big and bushy. If you make it slender, it will be fragile. After you have done a few of these, you can start playing around with different mustache treatments. For now keep it big. Run a stop cut along the top line of the mustache, and then carve down toward it. Be careful!

Lots of people carve off the mustache at this point. You want to leave the mustache on.

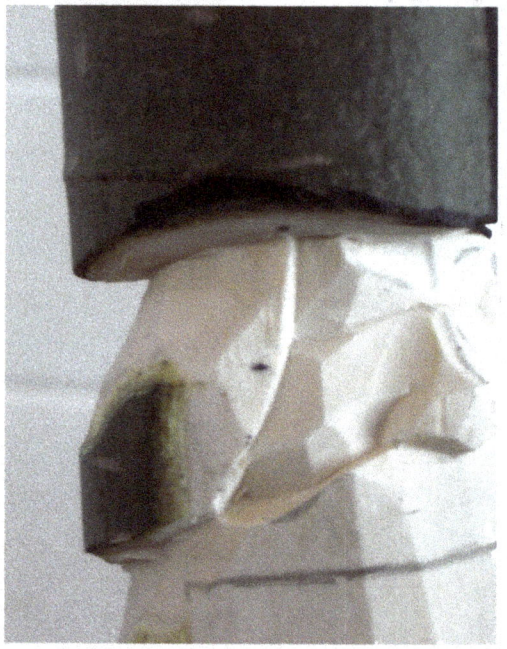

Then bevel the top of the mustache, right up to the nose, and nip off the chip as shown for a nice clean junction at this point.

~ Walking Sticks with Personality ~

Stop-cut along the straight line at the underside of the mustache, and then, using thumb push cuts *only*, clear out under the mustache. I emphasize thumb cuts because I have seen a lot of people make mistakes here that could have been avoided by following my advice.

As the whittlin' work gets more precise here, There are a few ways you might overdo the cuts here to the detriment of your final product, so proceed with care and read the instructions carefully before you start.

First, you'll want to avoid getting the beard area flat. Maintain the wedge shape under the mustache, and do not create the aforementioned orthodontic issues by cutting too deep here. It should be no deeper under the mustache than above it.

~ Walking Sticks with Personality ~

Now sketch and shape the underside of the mustache as shown.

When people (usually men!) with heavy mustachios keep their mouths shut, you usually can't see that they even have one under there.

But if you want to put a mouth in your whittlin', it is rather easy. Just make a couple of stop cuts right there at the V on the underside of the mustache and then clear out the chip, and there it is.

A lot of mustache talk! Moving on now.

Here is where we are. I have shaved the area below the beard down to a diameter which is comfortable to grasp. I did not make a hard line under the beard at this point, but some people do. It's really a matter of personal taste, depending on how you like your beard—or how your whittled man likes his in this case.

Now, that big lump of wood at the top of the head is destined to become a top hat and the following pages will show you how to do it.

~ Walking Sticks with Personality ~

Sketch in the top of the hat brim. Make it pretty thick to keep it strong while whittlin' on it.

~ Bushcraft Whittling ~

Then make a stop cut on that line and carefully whittle down toward the brim as shown.

The cuts must be controlled carefully to avoid cutting or splitting off the brim. Lots of small cuts. Keep deepening the stop cuts.

~ *Walking Sticks with Personality* ~

In this photo, I am using a cut that works by holding the knife kind of sideways in my fingers, bracing the thumb against the brim and then cutting by rotating the whole hand. I'm not pulling the blade toward the thumb. This is difficult to describe. The main thing is to NOT get in a hurry here. Keep your hands in safe positions and take lots of small cuts.

When making hats, take care to make the hat fit the head. It seems obvious, but a lot of whittled figures have hats that just look weird, because they are either very tiny or far too big and look like they are defying gravity! The front of the crown of the hat should line up with the forehead, and the sides of the crown should line up with the head. You did trim the hair mass down so that it would depict the hair mashed down by the hat, right?

Also, with this kind of a hat, and many other kinds, it is important that the top of the crown match the brim in its basic angle of the head. If it doesn't, it looks dumb.

I have this one right. Make yours right too.

I left a little bark on this head for accents, and if the stick had dried until the bark would really stick on, I could have left bark on the hat brim and the crown. This stick was too fresh though, and the bark was just falling off as I worked.

You can see that I carved detailed eyes on this guy too. Doing this is an entire chapter in itself (the next chapter, in fact). The instructions on eyes that I have outlined for the wood spirit will help you to depict acceptable eyes for this project. If you decide to attempt to carve eyes for this project, *please* first carve at least five eyes and then two or three pairs of eyes for practice in wood that is identical, and with identical grain orientation, to that in your stick. Do this before trying to put detailed eyes on your project. Practice does not really make perfect, but it does make things a lot better.

CHAPTER 8

~~~

Eyes

So here is that eye chapter for those who want to really add life to their caricatures and animal whittlin's.

In teaching people to whittle and carve, I find that this is where a lot of frustration happens. Here are some absolutely key points to keep in mind when doing eyes:

Your knife has to be sharp. No, really! Take the time to ensure that your knife is absolutely razor sharp and that you have a blade that is really pointy. Eyes are hard enough without the added handicap of a less-than-screaming sharp blade.

Make sure you can see what you are doing. Good light, and magnification if possible, and necessary. Being nearsighted, I find that it helps for me to take off my glasses to be able to see better close up.

THE EYES HAVE IT

Practice. You will not likely be doing good eyes until you have done several bad to average ones. More than 5. Maybe more than 10. After 20 or so there will be noticeable improvement. I am not kidding here. Do not give up.

No chewing! Every touch of the knife needs to be a cut, not a scrape or a pry.

Practice first on scrap wood of the same species and grain orientation as the finished carving. Here I am demonstrating on an aspen stick.

Do not attempt your first eye carving on your actual project. I know some of you will ignore this advice. You will regret ignoring it. I do not need the gift of prophecy to say this, only experience with beginning carvers. I do have a lot of that.

A sharp pencil is very helpful—actually essential.

Okay. Let's do this!

START OUT STRONG

First, whittle those two planes that intersect at about 90 degrees and then cut off that wedge that forms the top of the nose and the forehead. Make the stop cuts across the little corners and make the wide notches that form the sides of the nose and the eye socket.

~ Eyes ~

This method of making the eye socket will help to automatically have the eye tilted forward as it should be. If the lower lid of an eye is ahead of the upper lid, it will have a really strange look.

That stop cut in the middle of the notch will eventually become the lower lid of the eye. Notice that in this example it droops toward the outside.

If it does droop a bit, the face can look relaxed or even cheerful. If it droops a lot, the face will look sad or tired.

If higher on the outside than by the nose, it will look angry, maybe even evil. If it goes straight across, it will look, well, wooden. It is wood, but shouldn't look "wooden."

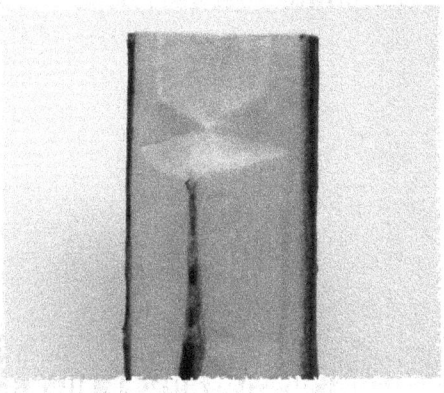

Sketch in the eye as shown. You can sketch in the other eye too, and while it is a good idea to practice doing both left and right eyes, do not be overly concerned with pairs of eyes for your first few attempts. Once you are happy with what you are doing with individual eyes, then work on pairs. Make them as big as you can.

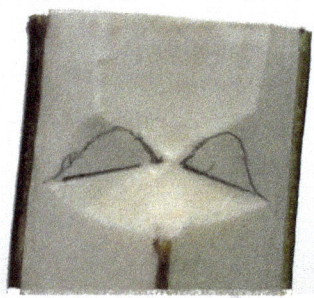

Now get your pointiest blade out. Did I mention that it needs to be sharp? I thought so. It is good if it is thin too.

~ *Eyes* ~

Make a stop cut straight into the wood along that arched line you created.

Then slice up toward that stop cut as shown . . .

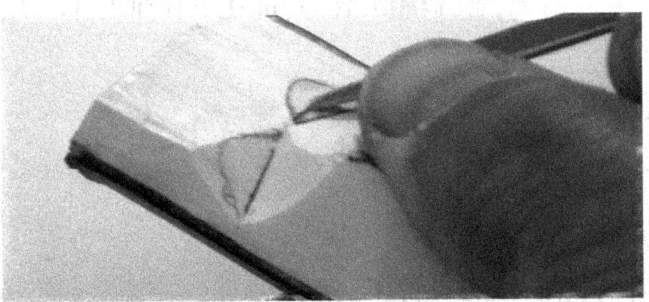

. . . to achieve this result. This will produce the top of the upper eyelid.

Sketch in the underside of that eyelid, and then carefully stop cut along that line. You'll want to start the stop cut in the corner of the eye and cut toward the middle, and then start again at the other corner and meet the first stop cut in the middle.

Cut lightly. Not deeply. Do not cut from the middle into the corner of the eye, lest you pull off the eyelid in the process. At some point in your practice you will do this wrong, and you will then know from experience why I say this.

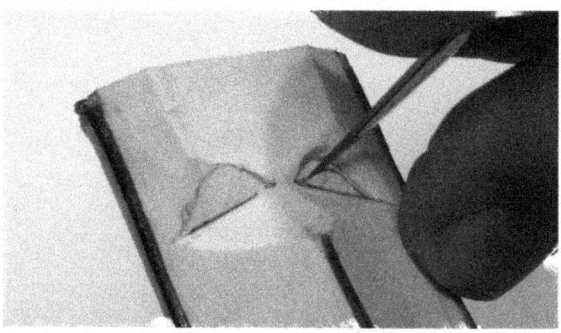

~ *Eyes* ~

Cut, or deepen, the straight line on the underside of the first eye, again starting in the corner and cutting to the center and then coming in from the other corner.

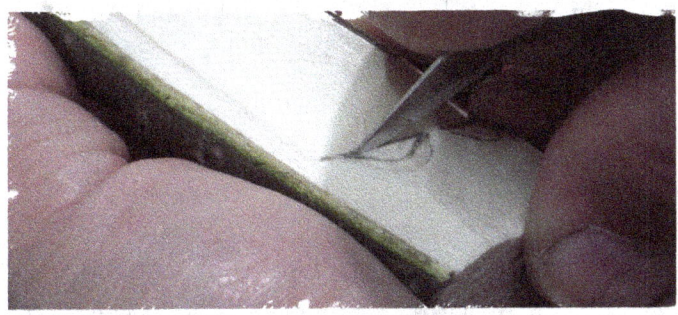

Now repeat on the other side, to make the other eye. Slight variations in shape will give the face a lopsided expression, so cut with care.

Now take a chip out of the corners and gently, carefully, round the eyeball slightly. More rounding should be evident from corner to corner than from top to bottom.

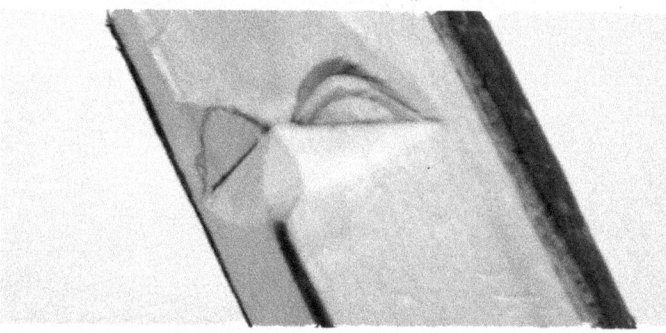

A little work shaping the lower lid and it's done!

~ Eyes ~

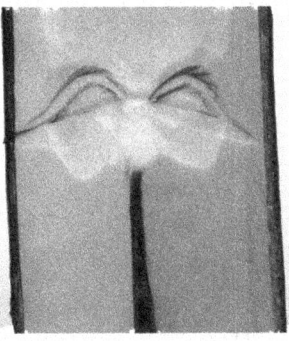

Do another one. And another. Do the other side. Try a matching pair or three.

If you put divots, as shown, into the eyes, it can appear that your figure is looking one way or the other. I almost never have my figures looking straight ahead.

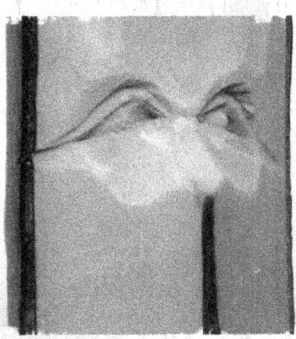

When you feel good about this, do it on a face that you have carved.

Follow the photos below to see the process on animal eyes. Pay attention to the specific shapes of the eyes in different creatures. When I do animal eyes, I don't carve in the eyelids.

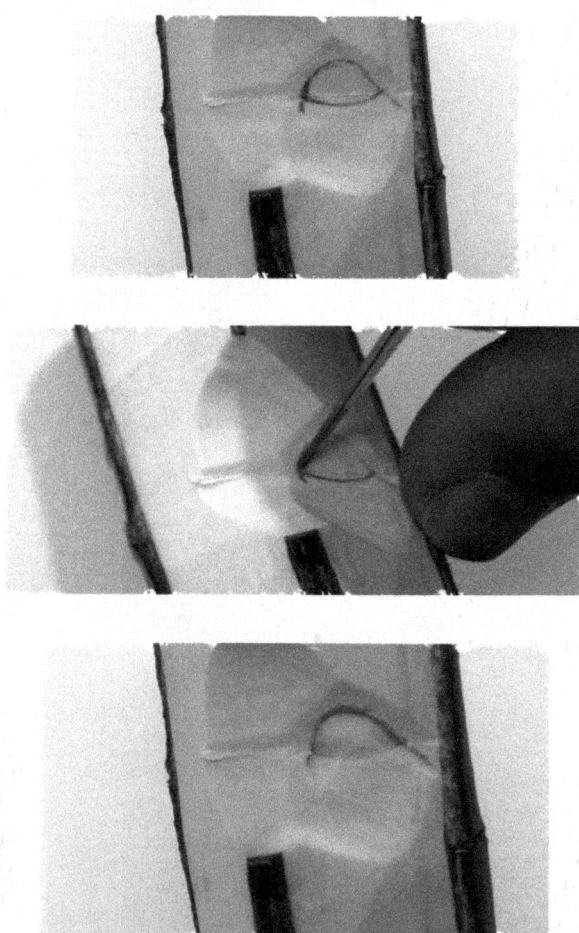

CHAPTER 9

~~~

Whittling Bushcraft Tools

The dingle sticks, pothooks, and spoons from earlier in the book could be called tools, but the projects in this chapter will go beyond them and be useful.

Shovel

Once I got my pickup truck stuck in the snow out in the bush. I didn't have a shovel with me. I did have a sharp axe though and a handy tree. In half an hour I had a serviceable shovel and got unstuck. It would have been better to have brought a metal shovel along, but this makes a better story! It was the first thing I ever made with that axe.

An 18" shovel is pretty handy around a campfire but kind of awkward to pack along. It isn't all that hard to make one with the axe, like this: Try to get a sound piece of wood about 6" in diameter. Hardwood is best. Alder, maple, birch, aspen, or poplar will work fine. Saw it to length. Split it down the middle. Hew it into a 1"-thick board. Axe whittle the handle down to size, sharpen the shovel end, and there! It is really just a big spatula. Shovels like this that are quite crude are still useful. The investment of more time can make them a lot nicer.

~ Bushcraft Whittling ~

~ *Whittling Bushcraft Tools* ~

~ Bushcraft Whittling ~

Exactly the same procedure can be used to make a paddle for a canoe. Originally, all paddles were made this way.

This shovel, or one like it, can be handy for other camping chores too. It is even useful to make one that resembles a garden trowel, to carry in your day pack for when a single-use latrine needs to be made. For this purpose, make it like a spoon, only heftier.

Mallet

When you need something to pound against an axe or knife to split a piece of wood, the usual approach is to simply grab a stick of firewood. The idea of pounding on an axe or a knife with another axe or a rock makes my skin crawl. Please do not even contemplate such brutality.

Using an axe to pound on another axe will seriously damage both axes. The stick works, but if a lot of this kind of thing is anticipated, it may be worthwhile to make a simple mallet, which will do a more efficient job and be easier to use, especially if it is being used on an axe.

Just get a little log, or round up a chunk of wood that is a little too big to comfortably hold in one hand and pound with. Using the axe, carefully thin down a handle. You might want to smooth the handle somewhat with a knife.

A mallet like this can be used to split wood very safely and accurately. With this system, two kids can split a lot of wood with considerably more efficiency and safety than using the axe in the traditional way.

~ Bushcraft Whittling ~

~ Whittling Bushcraft Tools ~

Quite large mallets like this can be made, if major pounding tasks are needed.

Here is the mallet in use:

Buck Saw

If a buck or bow saw is desired for a lot of wood processing, but you do not want to carry the big thing, it is quite possible to make a good saw out in the bush. Of course, you will need a saw blade, some strong cord, and a few nails. Actually, only two nails are needed, but Murphy's Law says that you better bring several. It is a lot easier to carry these parts than to carry an entire saw. Actually, I think the big folding saw that I have is superior to a buck saw, but your opinion might be different.

Here's how. Look at the photo to see the parts that will be needed:

Get some strong green wood. These are birch sticks about 1½" in diameter. The length will be determined by the length of the blade you have. This blade is 18" long, and the sticks are 16". Slightly longer sticks would work too. The spreader piece, that crosspiece in the middle, needs to be rather close to the length of the blade.

First make the rectangular holes, or mortices, in about the middle of the uprights. Make these first because it is easier to adjust the size of the ends of the crosspieces, or tenons, to fit the mortices than it is to make the holes the right size for the tenons.

Cut across the grain first. This will help to prevent splitting the stick. Do this part first; that way if you mess up, you will not have invested time on the slot for the blade on something that will be discarded. Do the hard part first and then the easy parts. Take your time, and maybe use the smaller blade of your pocketknife to help clean out the slot.

Then make the tenons fit. They don't have to be perfect or even particularly tight.

Use the saw blade to make slots in the ends of the uprights for the blade to fit. Whittle a notch so that the nails in the end of the blades won't allow the blade to slip out, and whittle a notch on the ends opposite the blade for the tensioning rope, as shown.

~ Bushcraft Whittling ~

Put the whole business together as shown, using a stick to twist the rope and put tension on the blade.

Now find something to saw!

The buck saw can be quickly broken down to make it into a compact package.

CHAPTER 10

~~~

Toys

Hot glue is useful for some of the projects in this chapter. Did you know the original hot glue was made by woodsmen long before there were any electrical gizmos and before bushcraft was even a word. Seriously.

Here's how to make it. First, get a can. An Altoids tin is perfect. Actually, get two cans or tins.

Collect pitch from pine, spruce, or fir trees into one of the tins. Use a stick for this if it is warm outside so that your fingers and knife don't get all sticky. If the weather is cool, maybe with some snow around, the pitch will be non-sticky and using the knife or hatchet will be fine.

I am collecting pitch from a Douglas fir with my axe in that first photo. Catch as much of the chipped-off pitch as you can with the can.

Also look around and find some old and dried deer or moose droppings and put them in the second can.

A moose was here!

Collect some cold but burned coals and put them in the second tin along with the moose manure.

Using a stick or maybe the little shovel you made, scrape a little pile of coals from the fire off to the side away from the

~ Toys ~

flames, so that you can work without getting too hot. This is a good time to have gloves on.

Put the tin on the coals so that the pitch can melt into liquid, and then mix in the charcoal/manure powder. This will turn the pitch mix black. You might want to slide the tin off the coals at this point.

Take a stick, ¼"–½" in diameter, and dip it in the melted pitch mix. Take it out and let it cool a bit, then re-dip and cool it repeatedly until all the melted pitch you can get has accumulated onto the stick.

Now to use the glue: just heat the glob until it begins to melt, using a lighter, candle, or fire, and then dab it onto

165

a surface you wish to glue. Then put the pieces to be glued together immediately—and it's done!

If you delay too long and the glue hardens before the pieces can be brought together, just warm up the pieces with some of the now-hardened glue on them and then put them together.

Having this glob of glue in a plastic bag in your pack is handy. It will always be available for little jobs and it can be activated quickly using a Bic-type lighter. It is, of course, possible to keep a tin of hardened mix available, but in that case a little fire will be needed to get some coals to melt the whole works, which is the way to go for larger jobs.

This "glue" is great for waterproofing things and is what was used to waterproof the seams in birch bark canoes. Someone reading the journals of the explorers who used these canoes in the 1700s and early 1800s will constantly encounter the phrase "gummed canoes," which refers to the application of this substance to places where the explorers' canoes were leaking. This application was needed a lot with birch bark canoes. Often several times per day. A pot quite a lot bigger than an Altoids tin full of the pitch mix was typically carried in the canoe for this purpose.

Warning! Do not attempt to heat the glue over an open flame. You will ignite the mix if you do.

It is easier, of course, to just bring along one or two glue sticks, such as those used in an electric hot glue gun. They can be used by melting the end with a burning stick from the fire or with a flame from a Bic-type lighter. You can either drip the melting plastic on the surface to be glued or dab the melted end of the glue stick on the surface to be glued. Put the items to be glued together immediately. If you don't work fast enough, it is possible to warm the pieces up again and stick them together when the glue melts.

The glue from the glue sticks will ignite, but that ignition is easy to blow out.

A really wonderful product that deserves mention is Shoe Goo. This is great stuff for fixing shoes and boots, for fixing leaks, and for gluing things together. It holds well, is not brittle, and is easy to take along in its tube. It does take a few hours to dry though.

Now let's take a look at some fairly simple toys that bushcrafters can make.

When I work with kids at summer camps, something I have done for many years, I am always whittlin' stuff to give to them. They love to see the items getting made and enjoy playing with them. I think it encourages them to know that someone cares about them enough to work on something for them.

Flying Propeller

For this project the firewood pile is a good place to look for material. A wide variety of species of wood will work fine. If it is good for the fire, it will be good for this. I try to avoid wood with sticky pitch. The piece in the photos is aspen, but birch, various kinds of pine, alder, and poplar will all work.

Size is not critical, but you can see from the following pictures what a good size might be.

As shown in the example here, I start by finding a piece of wood with straight grain and no knots, and split it down so that it is about 1½" x 1½", and then cut it to length so that it is about an inch or so longer than your bushcraft knife—in this case about 9" long.

Then split it down farther until you have one piece that is about ½" thick and about 1½" wide, and a couple of sticks of about ½" x ½".

~ Toys ~

Shorten the wide piece to about the length of the knife, and carefully whittle it into a little board about ¼" x 1". Make it nice and even, the same width and thickness over all.

Find the middle and mark it.

Make a hole in the middle. The easiest way is with the awl on your pocketknife, if your pocketknife is so equipped. The screwdriver on your multi-tool will also work. Do not stick the point of your knife into the little board and twist. The results of that will not be satisfying, and it is not safe.

If you need to use a knife blade for this, make a square hole. Draw a little square first, then make some across-the-grain cuts first, and then with-the-grain cuts. This will reduce the possibility of splitting your project. If you do split it, start again. Try to make a square hole about 3/16" by 3/16", or if using the awl or screw driver, a 3/16"-round hole. Work from only one side of the little board for this hole making, because that will produce a tapered hole that will make a better joint with the handle of the project later.

~ Toys ~

Now start fairly close to the hole and shave off the right top edge of the board, until it looks like this:

Flip it end for end and do the same on the other end. It is always the right corner that is shaved.

Note: If you wish to make a left-handed version, it is always the left top corner that is shaved. Left-handed ones are easier for lefties to make.

Now turn the board over and do the same thing to both ends on the other side, until it looks like this.

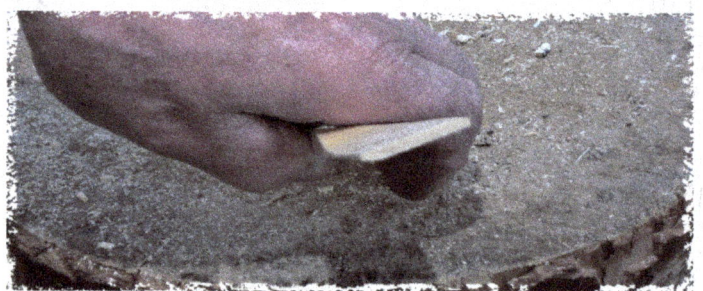

Round the sharp corners a bit. It will hurt less when you hit yourself in the face.

Take a look at your propeller and remember that the enemy of aviation is weight. Make that propeller as light as possible. It should be light and not clunky.

Now put your knife down on a firm surface with the edge up, and attempt to balance the propeller on it. Shave the heavy end until it teeters back and forth equally. It doesn't have to be perfect, but the closer to perfect the better.

Now whittle the stick that will be fitted to the hole.

For some reason, kids usually make these sticks too thin and weak, and adults tend to make them thick and heavy. Try to make a nice round stick about the thickness of a pencil. Save the fitting to the hole for last. That way if you destroy a stick or two getting to a good one, you won't have wasted your time and effort fitting a stick that will just get tossed.

The finished stick should be longer than the propeller. If the propeller is carved very evenly, you could get away with a stick that is the same length or shorter than the propeller, but most of these won't be all that perfect, and the longer stick dampens out the imperfections. If you find that your prop flops around in flight, try making a longer stick.

Now put the two together with a little bushcrafter's hot glue, or regular hot glue. Let that harden.

Hold the toy as shown, with the stick between the heel of the left hand and the fingertips of the right hand. Just push the right hand forward. If you didn't read these instructions carefully, you likely did it backward and it went down, not up! Almost everybody does it wrong at first. This might be experiential evidence of what theologians call "total depravity"!

Anyway, do it right and it works. Don't point it toward your face.

If you made a left-handed propeller, then of course you need to reverse the flying instructions.

Slip Bark Whistle

Let's make noise! If there is one thing kids love to do, it's making noise!

Here is how to make the classic slip bark whistle.

Be aware that this is a seasonally sensitive project. In most of North America and Europe, spring and early summer are the only times that the bark will slip. After about the second week of August, the season is over for me where I live in British Columbia. I have done this in September in Mexico though, so it is possible that in more tropical areas this could be done year round.

The easiest bush to work with for a whistle of this sort is willow. In fact, these gadgets are often referred to as "willow whistles." Lots of other trees and bushes will work too. In my part of the world, south central BC, the first bush that I have been able to use in the spring is what Canadians call the Saskatoon berry bush. People in the US call it serviceberry. Maples work, alders too, so experiment.

The photo below shows some important things. The part that you are going to make the whistle from needs to have about two inches of smooth bark. No buds branches or blemishes. The diameter of an adult finger thickness is about right.

Now this is very important: work so as to be taking the bark off the *top* of the branch. Notice that the branch stub left on (near the knife's tip) is pointing up. This is because all branches taper, being bigger toward the base and smaller toward the top.

If an attempt is made to take the bark off the branch toward the base, a small end of bark will have to stretch over a thicker piece of wood and that will lead to splitting the bark.

If at any time during this process the bark splits, it will be necessary to start again. This is a wonderful exercise in learning to cut cleanly with a sharp knife. A dull knife will make an awful mess of whistle attempts!

~ *Toys* ~

First whittle the top end of the section that will become the whistle, as illustrated. No tears or ragged bits of bark allowed! This has to be crisp. This is the mouthpiece.

Then about 1½" to 2" down the stick, make a clean one-line cut all around the stick. This cut has to go right through the bark and go all around the stick.

A lot of whistle-making failure happens right here. Take care to do it right.

Next, with the whistle blank laid on a firm smooth surface, tap the bark all over in the area between the mouthpiece end and the cut that was made all around the stick—this is the part of the bark that will need to be removed in order to whittle out the inside of the whistle.

Do not tap the bark anywhere else. It is important to tap the bark all over in the area where it will be removed. Use a closed pocketknife, particularly the smooth metal end of the handle (that part is called the "bolster" by the way). Random tapping in various places will not do it. Be careful! Tap it all over.

Sometimes it is helpful to peel the bark off another stick to use for tapping, and for carefully rubbing the bark that will be removed. The idea here is to bruise the inner bark enough to make it separate from the wood, but at the same time to avoid breaking it.

Then firmly grasp the whistle stick with both hands, one on the tapped part and one on the untapped area, and give it a twist. If the bark has been tapped/rubbed properly, you will hear a little pop, and the bark will come loose and can be slipped off the end of the wood with the thumb as shown.

~ Toys ~

If you grab and pull you will likely squish the bark tube and break it, so use your thumb.

It may take a few tries to figure out how hard to tap and rub so the bark will come loose without being broken. Don't give up! Just remember, if the bark is broken during this process, it will be necessary to start again.

Once you get the bark off, then put it right back on where it came from. On the top of the mouthpiece, about ½" from the end, make a stop cut through the bark and into the wood.

Don't let the bark slip out of position during this process. Then use a thumb push cut to clean out a notch, as shown.

Do not make this notch too large. Look at the photo for guidance. Clean and crisp cuts are very important here. In fact, the expression "clean as a whistle" refers more to the cuts necessary than it does to sanitation! By the way, wood is sanitary and has an amazing ability to kill germs.

Now slip the bark tube off with your thumb. Notice that there is a notch in the wood under the bark? This notch and, most importantly, the original stop cut that was made in forming it, will be your guide in making the sound chamber.

~ Toys ~

Deepen that stop cut. Make sure that the position of the stop cut remains the same throughout this process. It cannot be closer to the end of the whistle than it was when made originally, or the whistle won't work. Then using thumb push cuts, as shown, whittle out the sound chamber. Make it big enough. Use the photos for reference. Many beginner whistle makers make the sound chamber too small, and that may result in a whistle that is pitched so high that only dogs can hear it—and they won't tell!

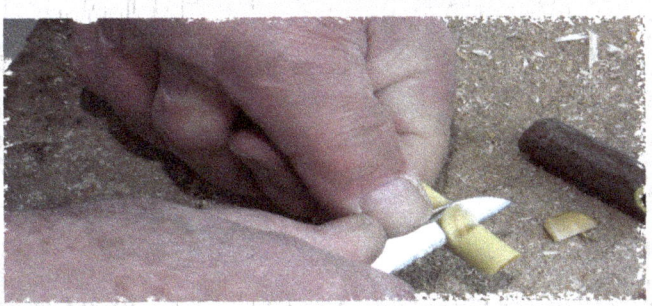

~ Bushcraft Whittling ~

There needs to be some uncarved wood left between the end of the sound chamber and the place where the cut was made all around the bark.

A little slice of wood needs to be taken off the top of the mouthpiece, so that air can be blown into the sound chamber. *Be careful!* You can lose it right here. This needs to be even and not too big. It can be made bigger if necessary, but you will not be able to make it smaller later.

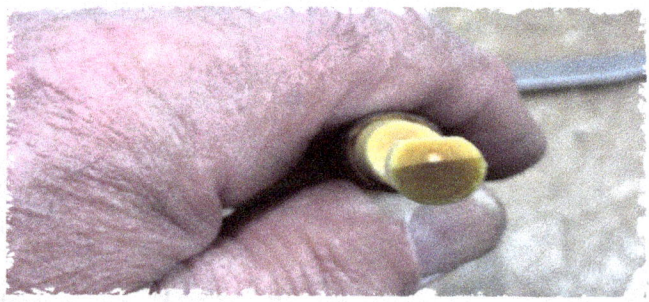

Put the bark back on, and blow. If it works, great. Make more! If it doesn't, try to figure out why. See how your attempt differs from the pictures and make improvements. Some people get this right off. Most have to make a few attempts but can learn a lot about precision whittlin' in the process.

Carefully whittle the whistle off the larger stick an inch or so beyond the cut through the bark.

Willow whistles will tend to stop working after a while as the bark dries out. In my experience, the ones made out of maple will work for years.

Bull Roarer

Another way to make noise is with what is called a "bull roarer."

This is a weird thing that is very easy to make. Apparently, it was used to communicate in ancient times by several primitive societies in widely separated areas of the world.

Start by getting a little log about 3" to 4" in diameter. The kind of wood is not important, though don't choose wood that is so hard that it will be difficult to work.

I am using a birch log here. By now you may have gotten the impression that I kind of like birch. Split it down the middle.

Then, by slitting and hewing, make a little board about ¼" thick.

Next, still using the axe (this is a good axe-whittlin' project by the way, since it can be pretty crude and still work fine),

~ Toys ~

give the board some shape. The exact shape is not important. All kinds of shapes will work.

Thin down the edges as shown here so that the board is thicker in the middle than at the edges and as even as you can make it.

Carefully make a hole in the board, far enough from the edge so that it doesn't chip out, and tie on some strong cord, 3' or so. I made a handle too, so that spinning it isn't quite so hard on the hands.

~ Toys ~

Find a place with some room and swing it around. It should start to spin on the end of the cord and give off a weird low-pitched noise. Changing the length of the cord will change the sound, and some users do just that while using it to do whatever communicating that the particular tribe has decided on for their code.

This has the potential to be a fun sort of a game for several participants.

Down Creek Racer

Here is a simple little toy that also can be pretty crude but still be a lot of fun—especially if there are a few people participating so it can become a competition.

These are just little boats that can hold a pebble and can be floated down a stream. Participants can agree on some design parameters such as size. When the boats are finished, a pebble is placed in them and they are all launched. Once sent on their way, no one is allowed to touch their boats. If they get stuck, they can only be freed by throwing rocks or sticks. When a boat loses its pebble, the owner has to stand at that point of the stream until the last boat has lost its stone.

College-age young people have been, in my experience, totally consumed for hours by this simple game on a hot day in the mountains.

Any piece of wood can be used to make the boat, which can be of any configuration that the participants agree to.

Here I am going to show a little canoe made out of cottonwood bark. The thick material, up to 4" in some cases, is almost as easy to carve as soap and has a beautiful grain. I often carve human and animal caricatures out of it.

Square up a piece of bark with axe and knife, sketch out the shape of the canoe, and whittle the outside shape. Then using the gouge or bent knife that was used to make a spoon, hollow out the inside.

There is absolutely no question that this will float, but some extra whittlin' might be necessary to get it to float right and to win!

Projects for bushcraft whittlin' could go on forever! There is just no end to the possibilities. As long as the tools are there, and the materials (rarely in short supply!), there is endless opportunity for fun with bushcraft whittlin'.

Don't wait until you get to the bush! I have done bushcraft whittlin' in many nonforest environments such as the Arizona desert, suburbia, and in urban centers like Brisbane, Australia, where on a walk I encountered trees being trimmed in a park. A gold mine! If you look, branches, sticks, and scrap wood are to be found in a lot of places that you might not expect to find them.

Grab them and have fun. Happy whittlin'!

About the Author

Rick Wiebe has been whittling for over 60 years and still has a full complement of working fingers.

He carves many different kinds of projects: walking sticks with animal heads, human caricatures, and large log projects using chain saws and more. His pieces are in private collections worldwide.

Rick teaches whittling and carving to children ages nine and up, and to adults too, in many different venues including clubs, schools, homeschool groups, community recreation programs, and private sessions.

He and his wife of 48 years live in Westbank, BC, and work with Mobile Missionary Assistance Program (mmap.org) in the southern US during the winter. He often gets to carve as part of this work too.

Rick and Helen sell carving tools at woodcarvingbiz.com, where a gallery of some of his work can be seen.

More from whittling master Rick Wiebe

Whittlin' Whistles
How to Make Music with Your Pocket Knife

ISBN: 978-1-610350-49-5
PRICE: $12.95
PAGES: 64
FORMAT: Paperback

One of the signature projects whittlers enjoy working on is the whistle, and this book addresses each and every detail of successful whistle making. With a pocket knife and some readily available materials, beginning carvers will produce fun and attractive whistles that they can show off to their friends.

Linden Publishing / WoodworkersLibrary.com

More from whittling master Rick Wiebe

Classic Whittling
Basic Techniques and Old-Time Projects

ISBN: 978-1-610352-54-3
PRICE: $14.95
PAGES: 136
FORMAT: Paperback

In *Classic Whittling*, author Rick Wiebe—a whittler for more than 60 years—provides the fundamentals for anyone looking to learn this classic craft. *Classic Whittling* begins with the basics of a good knife and how to keep it sharp and then moves into an array of fun projects. By the end of *Classic Whittling*, your knife will become a magic wand that turns firewood into fun and fascinates your family and friends.

Linden Publishing / WoodworkersLibrary.com

www.ingramcontent.com/pod-product-compliance
Lightning Source LLC
Chambersburg PA
CBHW042138160426
43200CB00020B/2969